SEA ANGLING
from
Kent to Cornwall

Edited by Mel Russ

Stanley Paul
London Sydney Auckland Johannesburg

Stanley Paul and Co. Ltd

An imprint of Random Century

20 Vauxhall Bridge Road,
London SW1V 2SA

Random Century Australia (Pty) Ltd
20 Alfred Street, Milsons Point, Sydney 2061, Australia

Random Century New Zealand Limited
191 Archers Road, PO Box 40–086, Glenfield, Auckland 10

Century Hutchinson South Africa (Pty) Ltd
PO Box 337, Bergvlei 2012, South Africa

First published 1990

Copyright © Mel Russ, 1990

Set in 10/11½ pt Century Light

Printed and Bound in Great Britain by Butler and Tanner Ltd.
Frome and London

British Library Cataloguing In Publication Data
  Sea angling: a guide from Kent to Cornwall
  1. Great Britain. Sea angling
  1. Russ, Melvyn
  799.1′60941

ISBN 0 09 174244 7

CONTENTS

To explore the coastline more fully, use the Landranger Series of maps published by Ordnance Survey (1:50 000).

Kent – 178, 179 and 189
Sussex – 199, 198 and 197
Hampshire – 196 and 195
Dorset – 195, 194 and 193
Devon – 192, 202 and 201
Cornwall – 201, 204 and 203

Mel Russ

INTRODUCTION

SEA angling is an exciting sport. Being out in the open air, close to the coast, able to see the marine environment change from minute to minute, and try the ultimate test – to catch a fish – makes angling a unique 'personal' experience.

For the fisherman living close to the sea these things are almost an everyday common occurrence. For the rest of us, and especially those living miles from the coast, we can but occasionally 'dip in' to what's happening along the shoreline and out to sea.

Lots of anglers simply aren't tapped into the angling grapevine and their only means of picking up information is to regularly read the specialist angling press or talk to coastal-based tackle dealers.

This book is aimed at bringing a mountain of information to the angler who wants instant help on a particular fishing region – whether he be a shore angler or a man who likes to catch his fish afloat.

That's why I have pulled a team of writers and top-class anglers together – their brief to explain to you what is happening on their particular stretch of the coast.

I have picked the English Channel counties of Kent, Sussex, Hampshire, Dorset, Devon and Cornwall because they are not only prime fishing areas – but holiday centres as well. So it doesn't matter if you are a keen angler, a beginner or just a casual holiday 'dipper' – everything within these covers will help you catch more fish and, more importantly, help you enjoy your fishing.

You will note that I have omitted the Isle of Wight in this guide. There are several reasons for this. For a start the people living on the island know how to fish, and know where the fish are. Secondly, you have to get a ferry to the island – and they are very busy in summer – so casual angling sorties to the 'Wight' are few and far between. And, finally, I suspect that those holiday-makers who do visit the island don't, in general, go to fish.

You will find each of the six main sections follows the same format. This is to help you find the information you want more quickly. Each opens with an introduction to the county, which is to help you understand it better. Then there's an in-depth section on the tackle needed to fish the region's beaches; you will find some overlap here, although the complete range of shore and boat rigs are to be found within the book.

The next major section is a complete guide to the shore fishing in the county. This is followed by information on boat tackle and, finally, the guide to the boat fishing marks.

I hope you make use of this unique guide and find the fish in a feeding mood. Finally, a vote of thanks must go to the team of local experts who have made this book possible.

MEL RUSS is currently editor of the successful monthly *Sea Angler* magazine, and sister publication *Sea Angling Quarterly*, both published by the Peterborough-based EMAP Pursuit Publishing Company.
Prior to that he spent over ten years with IPC's *Angler's Mail*, working on both the news and features desks.
A keen all-round angler – with a passion for sea angling – he confesses to being hooked on the sport for over 30 years.

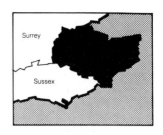

Alan Yates

KENT

ENGLAND International and top match angler
Alan Yates, who lives near Dover, reveals how to
fish the shore and boat marks around the Kent
coast.

SHELTERED ANGLING ALL YEAR ROUND

KENT is a county steeped in history. With its closeness to the Continent there has been a centuries-old connection with smuggling, while its marshes are the home of the famous Romney sheep.

But it is the fishing that we are more interested in here, and without doubt, the sea angler scores, for the county can offer beginner and expert alike some of the finest mixed fishing to be found anywhere around the British Isles.

Within its 80-mile coastline there are piers, cliffs, rocks, estuaries and storm beaches to fish from and there's a wide variety of fish to catch as well. And the great bonus − no matter how hard the wind blows, and from whatever direction, the sea angler can choose his venue carefully and continue fishing despite poor conditions elsewhere along the Channel.

Kent is situated on the far south-east tip of England and is as close as you can get to mainland Europe, just 21 miles of sea separates Dover from Cap Gris Nez, France. This narrow strip of water, the Straits of Dover, is where the English Channel and North Sea meet to become the busiest and most dangerous shipping lane in the world.

For the boat angler there are many dangers and the Straits of Dover, with its strong tides and twin shipping lanes criss-crossed by countless Channel ferries, is not the place for the novice angler. However, for angling in general the funnel effect of sea and tide through the Straits presents a concentration of resident and migratory species of fish within a small sea area.

Two world wars have resulted in a cluster of war-time wrecks of varied sizes, all within easy reach of the boat angler. Despite many of the wrecks being blown apart because they were a shipping hazard, many still hold large shoals of cod, pollack, pouting and big conger. Over 100 wrecks are to be found within ten miles of Dover and Folkestone alone.

Other attractions for the boat angler are the many sandbanks found throughout the Straits of Dover and North Kent coast with the Varne Bank and Goodwin Sands being the most famous.

The county can be split into two specific angling areas, with the deeper south coast the most productive for both boat and shore angling, especially during the winter months, when cod are the target species. The shallower, North Kent coast enjoys excellent sport in the spring and summer and is especially suited to inshore dinghy fishing for bass, thornback rays and smoothhounds.

Tides are generally strong in the English Channel and flow west to east during the flood and east to west during the ebb. The south coast offers better shore and boat fishing during the stronger flood tide, although around Deal and Thanet the shoreline responds better on the ebb flow. Along the north coast the shoreline is much shallower and tides are not so strong until you reach the Thames estuary, where the ebb flow is particularly powerful. Tides washing the North Kent coast are reversed, with the flood going east to west and the ebb west to east.

By far the most productive weather conditions along the shore follow a westerly or south-westerly gale, although the North Kent coast responds to a north-westerly on occasions. South-west is the predominant wind direction, and whilst this suits the shore-based angler, when the wind is blowing hard, it restricts boat movement from ports like Dover, Folkestone and Dungeness. A light north-westerly wind favours the boat angler from these venues.

Whilst both boat and shore fishing is excellent throughout the seasons, Kent offers winter cod fishing second to none. Cod are to be found around the northern end of the English Channel all year round, but during the autumn and winter months shoals of cod from other sea areas converge and overlap, and from October through until February cod are landed in large numbers by both boat and shore anglers. Other winter species include whiting, pouting, dabs and flounders.

During the spring and summer the number of Channel species multiplies dramatically, and depending on the sun, air and water temperatures just about every species associated with British sea angling can be caught in the Straits of Dover. Even sharks are regular visitors to the Kent coast and, in fact, the British thresher shark record was held by a fish of 280 lb caught off Dungeness in 1933. Other summer species include bass, which are regular visitors between April and December.

The conger, for so long absent from the Kent shoreline, is making a comeback and fish of 30 lb plus are now well within reach of the boat angler from July onwards. Other seasonal visitors include mackerel, which arrive from June onwards, smooth-hounds, which show from April, and plaice from May. There is also a marked spring codling run from February onwards after the sprat shoals and the breeding urge have attracted the bigger cod away into the North Sea. The spring codling can be caught from the rocks of Thanet through to Dungeness with the hours of darkness providing the best results in clear water.

The shoreline is constantly changing with the number of people living near the coast continuing to increase as the opening of the Channel Tunnel nears and we have closer ties with Europe. Plans to build marinas will mean better facilities for boats and anglers, although some previously popular shore angling spots are under threat. Cliff protection schemes and land reclamation all contribute to the shoreline changes, with new promenades at Thanet, Dover and Folkestone all adding to greater angling access.

The large population explosion does have its drawbacks, though, including the enormous angling pressure put on fish stocks in the region. The increase in pollution from sewage outfalls has also had its effect, with several species being driven away from the shoreline in recent years.

The once prolific dogfish is now rarely caught from the shore, although it is still taken by the boats fishing offshore. For the shore angler the more mundane species like pouting, silver eel, dabs, whiting and flounder are often the bread and butter of angling, and catching the more attractive species like plaice, sole, bass, rays and mullet isn't as easy as it was.

Tackle and techniques for fishing the Kent shoreline

WITH such a variety of species and varied coastline, the tackle required to fish the Kent coast covers the complete range from beachcasting to spinning. However, most anglers who fish from the shore concentrate on the bottom-feeding species with the cod high on their list.

A standard 12- to 13-foot beachcaster of fibreglass, carbon or Kevlar will prove more than adequate for the majority of the shore fishing available. Popular rods among Kent anglers come from the Zziplex factory based in New Romney, although other makes, such as Conoflex, Century and Daiwa, prove equally efficient for the sort of fishing found in the county.

There is an emphasis on light-weight pendulum rods for long-distance casting, because venues such as Seabrook, Hythe or Dungeness don't respond to short-range tactics. Rods capable of casting up to 6 oz are generally needed for fishing the South Kent beaches and piers, where strong tides are often encountered, although a lighter 4 oz casting blank will work perfectly well along the estuary areas of the North Kent coast and from the many piers such as Deal or the Prince of Wales Pier at Dover.

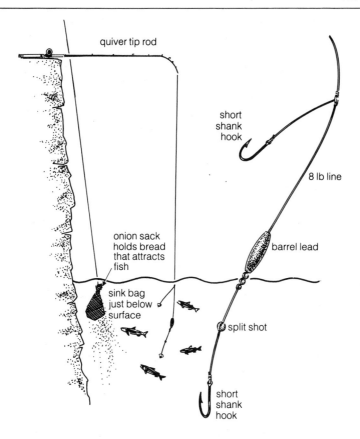

Figure 1 Mullet rig

Only two Kent venues demand a heavier rod and they are Dover Breakwater and Dungeness Point, where an 8 oz grip lead may be required to hold bottom in the strongest spring tide. A light 8- to 10-foot coarse angler's quiver tip rod is a useful addition if you wish to go for the grey mullet, which can be found around pier walls in summer.

A 10-foot spinning rod can be similarly used to fish for mackerel, garfish, pollack, scad and, in ideal calm conditions, bass. It is emphasised, though, that the two latter rods will not cope with general pier or beach angling and are only required for the specific species mentioned.

The two most commonly used reels are the multiplier and the fixed-spool, and the choice between the two is dependent on the angler. The multiplier is far more common on the Kent venues than the easier-to-use fixed-spool. Shore anglers prefer the multiplier because it fits the job and looks the part rather than because it is a better reel. Improved quality in both models in recent years has seen great strides in the distance they can be cast if loaded and handled correctly.

The fixed-spool reel offers the beginner tangle-free casting from the outset and a single model is better suited to a wider range of line sizes. The multiplier gives an easier to obtain maximum casting range once overruns are mastered.

Two different types of fishing are encountered along the Kent shore and these require not only a different angling approach but different reels. They involve distance casting over clean-bottomed beaches or fishing over heavy kelp and rocks. The former is best approached by using a small multiplier, such as an ABU 6500GR, 7000, Daiwa 6HM or Shimano FS11, loaded with 15 lb line and a short length of 60 lb shock leader. With this outfit the shore angler can cast a bait up to 150 yards.

A word of warning though – by reducing the line breaking strain, and therefore diameter, the shore angler is able to cast farther, but going below 15 lb breaking strain line is not practical. For rock fishing or indeed fishing any other snaggy ground or amongst floating weed, a heavier breaking strain line is required. This is usually 30 lb nylon fished straight through without a casting shock leader. The shock leader knot can often fill with weed and jam in the tip ring.

Reels preferred for this strength of line include the ABU 7000 C, seven, eight and nine, the Daiwa SL20 and the Shimano FS11 and FS111. In the case of fixed-spool reels several models are preferred and these can be used with spare spools loaded with the different breaking strains of line. Preferred models include the DAM 50001, Mitchell 486 and the Shimano Biomaster GT8000.

The remaining basic tackle includes a robust tackle box to keep tackle dry, plastic being best, and a rod rest to stand the rod on when fishing from the beach. A tripod rod rest is often preferred because it can be used anywhere, including the miles of concrete promenades that are a feature of the Kent coast. A tripod can also be adjusted to raise or lower the rod-tip height, thus getting the tip out of the wind or low enough to be watched without getting a stiff neck. Monopod rod rests have their uses in a storm to get the line high above the waves or when fishing from sand to keep the reel clean. An umbrella is an essential item of tackle because it keeps the angler dry and therefore warmer, whilst also providing cover and shade for expensive bait in warm weather.

What goes on the end of the line is perhaps the most critical

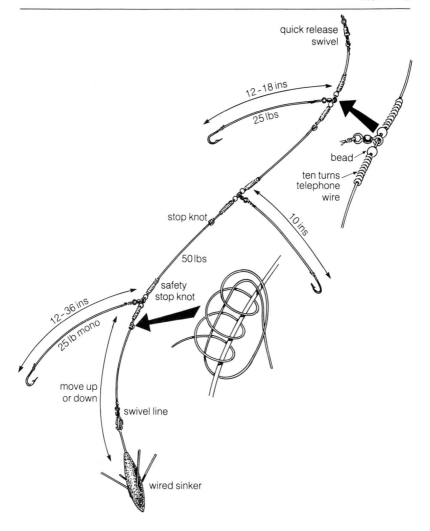

quick release
swivel

12-18 ins

25 lbs

bead

ten turns
telephone
wire

10 ins

stop knot

50 lbs

safety
stop knot

12-36 ins

25 lb mono

move up
or down

swivel line

wired sinker

Figure 2 Standard beach rig

area, and this includes both terminal tackle and bait. In the case
of the terminal rig, simplicity is the key and whilst complicated
terminal rigs may look the part on dry land they invariably
tangle in the sea. Tackle should present bait in an efficient,
tangle-free manner, whilst bait presented on the hook should not
impede the hook's performance.

The most successful terminal rig used in Kent is the simple
paternoster, with up to three hooks spaced equally up the body.

Variations include a longer snood on the lower hook in the form of a flowing trace from the same line as your leader, in most cases 50 lb to 60 lb breaking strain. Hook snoods should be of 25 lb breaking strain. It is a mistake to go for lighter snoods as they spin in the tide or quickly get damaged wafting about on the seabed.

The make-up of the rig is dependent on what the angler is fishing for. A single 3/0 or 4/0 hook rig is often preferred for cod and bass, while multi-hook rigs, with up to three size 1 to 4 hooks, are best for flatfish, whiting and pouting. A single bait rig for bass or cod can incorporate a Pennell twin hook system, which is especially effective for fishing large peeler crab or squid baits. Rigs made up with strong swivels stopped by telephone wire, beads or stop knots allow for adjustment of snood positions. Use only quality swivels on your rigs – Berkley is one of the best.

Most of the general baits work along the Kent shore throughout the year, although there is a marked difference in some venues between what the fish will accept on rocks or sand. For instance, it is very rare for a Kent bass to take lugworm from the rocks,

Figure 3 Pennell hook rig

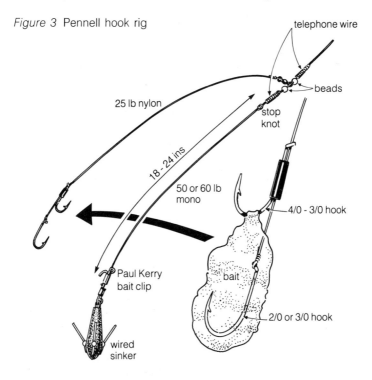

telephone wire

25 lb nylon

beads

stop knot

18 - 24 ins

50 or 60 lb mono

4/0 - 3/0 hook

Paul Kerry bait clip

bait

2/0 or 3/0 hook

wired sinker

although it does occasionally catch from the sandy beaches. Similarly, cod can be taken from the Kent rocks on peeler crab whilst from the sandy beaches of Dungeness it is rarely successful.

From May through the summer one of the most effective baits along the North Kent coast is live peeler crab, which is also effective throughout the winter months from Thanet, Deal and Folkestone rock marks for cod and codling. This is despite the fact that crab is not found locally and has to be imported from Devon! Frozen peeler crab is also highly effective during the winter months. Peeler crabs can be collected from the North Coast from May onwards, with a mass moult of crabs up until June – crabs are found in the mud and water pools between Gravesend and Thanet, where it is possible to pick up 100 per tide.

Lugworm is the commonest bait, with the yellowtail variety, which is dug from Sandwich Bay, one of the most deadly. Other lugworm on sale in tackle shops or dug locally include the Dungeness 'black' variety, which are simply yellowtails which have been gutted, and the common soft or blow lugworm, which is dug from Pegwell Bay, Whitstable and Seasalter. Other successful worm baits include king ragworm, with the small worms being excellent for flatfish and pollack in summer, and harbour ragworm, which are an excellent bait for flounders, pollack, bass and mullet from the piers.

Harbour ragworm, or 'Maddies', can be dug in the Stour estuary, Folkestone harbour and along the North Kent coast at Herne Bay and Reculver. Another worm bait which gives exceptional results from the beach is the white ragworm. 'Whites' come into their own during autumn and early spring, when they are deadly for codling, whiting, pouting and small flatfish. King and white ragworm can be dug in limited numbers from the North Kent coast, including the Isle of Grain, Isle of Sheppey, Whitstable and Herne Bay during the lowest spring tides.

A lesser-known worm bait, but nevertheless highly effective, is the rock worm, which can be dug from the chalk rocks all around the coast, with Thanet's Cliff Bays the ideal place to dig the worms using a small pick.

Other baits that find success, although on a limited scale, are squid and fish strip. They are most successful when used in cocktail fashion to tip off a lugworm bait. Best of the fish baits is sprat, which is excellent for winter whiting and dabs. Mackerel heads or whole fillets are ideal for pier bass from Dover Breakwater as are whole squid for the bigger specimens. In the main, though, fish baits are far less effective than worms. Shellfish such as razorfish, butterfish and queen cockles all have their day.

Guide to Kent's all-year beaches

IT could be argued that **Gravesend** is the nearest shore angling venue to London, which is probably why it gets a lot of attention from fishermen. Sited on the south shore of the Thames estuary, Tilbury is on the opposite Essex bank, about a mile across the river. Catches are limited to flounders and eels with the occasional bass or mullet in summer and cod, whiting and flounders in winter.

Shore angling in the area is hampered by muddy banks, and after rain these banks can be treacherous. Easy access and comfortable fishing can be found at **Greenhithe** promenade and **Gravesend** promenade, although catches are limited to eels and flounders. This area is especially noted as being ideal and safe for both junior and disabled anglers. During winter the stretch of shoreline adjacent to the **Gravesend Sea School** is popular because there is the chance of a 15 lb cod. This length of shoreline stretches two miles to **Shornmead Fort** and the **Shorn Light** and a top mark is the Black Post half-way along the venue.

Fishing is best over the high water with spring tides best. The ebb is particularly strong and a grip lead is required to hold bottom. Top baits throughout the Sea School stretch are lugworm, peeler crab and king and harbour ragworm, with boiled shrimp a local favourite for the flounders. The banks of the river are protected by a rocky wall which stretches out some 50 feet — a trap for grip leads if you don't reel in fast enough.

The **Isle of Grain** is a flounder angler's paradise, with lots of inlets and creeks in which to drop a ragworm or peeler crab bait. It is a comparatively shallow area and winter results show only the very occasional cod. Marks at **Higham Marshes**, **Allhallows**, **Yantley Creek** and **The Flats** down to **Hoo**, on the Medway estuary, all offer flounders. Best results come at high water: beware of the mud. Access is via the A228 from Rochester, and the B2001 to Grain.

There's lots of potential around the **Isle of Sheppey**, where shore catches have included thornback ray, smoothhounds and stingray. Even tope have been caught in the past. Nowadays, though, it enjoys only a shadow of its former glory, and sport majors on flounders and eels. When the sun shines in June or July and temperatures rise there's the chance of bass, smoothhound and thornback being taken from **Eastchurch Gap**, **Warden Point** or **Leysdown** on peeler crab.

For the remainder of the year the good old flounder can be

A favourite venue on the North Kent coast – the new promenade at Sheppey

found all around the island, with the **Westminster Wall, Swale** estuary at **Kingsferry, Rushenden Bay** and **Queenborough** amongst the favourite marks. During the spring, peeler crab, which is found all around the island, is the only bait worth using and this secures the odd decent bass as well as the flounders and eels.

A favourite bass mark is **Garrison Point**, on the north-west tip of the island, at the entrance to the River Medway. Strong tides make this mark difficult to fish, but it offers a chance of big bass, especially at night during midsummer. Sheppey's front beaches offer whiting and codling in winter during spring tides with **Barton Point** and the new promenade at **East End** top marks. Best baits are common or yellowtail lugworm, king and white ragworm, and peeler crab. Ideal conditions of a northerly onshore wind may offer much, but the island never guarantees anything.

Anglers are warned that the cliffs in the area around **Warden Point** are especially dangerous in wet weather and always likely to subside. The Isle of Sheppey can be reached via the M2 (take the A249 at junction 5).

The **Tankerton** to **Margate** stretch of shoreline offers comparatively limited fishing from the shore and is better known for its abundance of different types of bait. **Tankerton, Whitstable, Herne Bay** and **Reculver** offer eels and flounders in summer with the occasional bass or the odd stingray at **Bishopstone Rocks**. Herne Bay pier is only a shadow of its former self with the short stumps left after the original pier was demolished. It has, however, yielded double-figure cod in the depths of winter following onshore gales as well as whiting, dabs, flounders, plaice and the odd stingray.

Reculver, and its famous Roman remains, is fished regularly with its Towers landmark and car park more of an attraction than the fishing. Results are limited to flounders, rockling, eels and pouting in summer, with the odd stingray, bass or thornback over the low water to peeler crab or ragworm baits.

In winter codling and whiting are taken from the promenade over the high water at night with the **Cold Harbour Sluice** end of the venue best. **Birchington** to **Margate** offers similar sport in winter and summer with Birchington a noted eel mark during spring. Much of the previously inaccessible cliffs towards Margate are now bounded by a promenade and offer easy-access eel, bass and flounder fishing during spring and summer. There's bass and eels in summer and cod in winter over the low water up period from marks at **Minnis Bay, Beresford Gap** and **Epple Bay**, although results vary from year to year. Throughout the area between Tankerton and Margate peeler crabs are plentiful through the early spring and can be found alongside the groynes in the mud and under every rock or in every pool.

Whilst not a true island, **Thanet** is Kent's 'nose', which juts into the northern end of the English Channel. Thanet is where Kent's fishing 'proper' begins, for here we say goodbye to flounders and eels as the main species and meet bass, cod and a host of others.

Thanet offers rock fishing galore, with lots of chalk rocks and ledges from which to cast a peeler crab or lugworm bait. The mass of kelp and chalk boulders is a haven for the fish, which are within easy casting range. In fact, there are occasions when you need to do no more than lower your bait into a gully. The area around Thanet hosts seven chalky bays and each offers a different angle to the wind, which means there is always a sheltered venue to fish, no matter what the weather. **Palm Bay, Botany Bay, Kingsgate Bay, Joss Bay, Stone Gap, Viking Bay** and **Dumpton Gap** are all favourite angling marks, although not for the faint-hearted. Expect to lose tackle, while the danger of stepping into a deep gully or hole in the chalk rock is ever present.

At the Botany Bay end of the venue is **Foreness Point**, where a longfall sewer pipe stretches out to sea, giving anglers a vantage point to reach the bass shoals. This is also an ideal area to collect edible-type peeler crabs during July and September. The most productive fishing time is two hours either side of low water, although with new promenades being built around the base of the cliffs the previously unfishable high-tide period can now be fished and does vield results. In recent years the bass have declined around Tnanet because of the number of monofilament gill nets; now a single bass is a prized fish.

I remember catching six bass for 29 lb when an onshore northerly wind saw the bass feeding in earnest on peelers. I took the fish in consecutive casts from a rock outcrop at Botany Bay, and the secret of my success was casting accurately into a gully into which the fish were funnelling to feed. Such marks as **Killicks Hole** and the **Platform** offer unique cod fishing at close range, although there's an element of danger on the rocks.

At the southern tip of Thanet is the town of **Ramsgate**, with its large harbour protected by two piers. The harbour itself offers summer mullet fishing with the inside of the **Eastern Arm** being favourite, fished with bread and a bread bag from July through until November. The piers themselves offer the usual eels and flounders along with pouting, plaice, dabs, pollack and codling. Both offer free fishing. Best results come either side of the high water.

To the south of the Sally Line Ferry Terminal there's **Western Undercliff**, which offers easy access to the angler who likes to fish from the car. A narrow winding road reaches down to the promenade, where bass, flounders, codling, eels, pouting and rockling can be caught in season. Peeler crab is one of the best baits throughout summer with lugworm, rockworm, white ragworm and king ragworm all good alternatives.

Pegwell Bay is the large sandy bay below Thanet and has little or no angling interest because of its shallow nature. It does, however, offer excellent bait digging for common and yellowtail lugworm. A half-circle moat dug with a flat-tined potato fork open at the sea end drains off excess water. It's then possible to lift 300 lug per tide.

Famous for its yellowtail lugworm, **Sandwich Bay** is accessible only via the Sandwich Bay Estate toll road. Daily toll tickets in summer are £2.50 per car, whilst a season ticket is £17.50. The bay is shallow at its eastern end and deeper at its western end – consequently the best fishing is at the latter end, although the shallows do offer excellent sport with eels, flounders and the odd bass in the summer.

During the winter months best results come from the **Sandwich Bay Yacht Club** end of the bay, with cod to 30 lb having been landed. From October onwards dabs, sole, plaice, pouting, whiting, eels, flounders, codling and cod are caught regularly with low water as productive as high, provided it is dark. Farther west is **Sandown**, which fronts the Royal Cinque Ports Golf Club and is reached via the potholed extension of Golf Road. This is a private road which follows the path of the ancient highway between Deal and Sandwich.

Sandown comes into its own in winter with codling being caught at very short range over high water. Indeed, long casting is not necessary here and the venue is ideally suited for those anglers with limited casting skills. Half-way along the road is an ideal angling base, the **Chequers Inn**, which has a large car park at its rear within 150 yards of the beach. Top baits all year at Sandwich Bay and Sandown are yellowtail lugworm.

Deal is always wet and windy; perhaps that's why it's such a good place for shore fishing. I live there and conditions are always ideal; overcast, pea soup sea and a stiff breeze. Its situation on the corner of Kent must be to blame for its weather and, unlike many of the other Kent towns, Deal lacks sheltering hills. It's bleak in winter with its steep shelving beaches offering little protection for the angler − even the wooden groynes are few and far between. But what it lacks in comfort it makes up for in cod and codling.

The complete length of the shore between **Sandown** and **Walmer**, to the west, offers cod, especially in darkness over a peak ebb tide. Top bait is peeler crab, which has a certain magic compared to other baits in the region. It is so good that I will not fish Deal without it. Frozen peeler is as good as fresh in winter. Deal has its popular fishing marks, although they tend to be close to car parks or landmarks, and indeed the beach is excellent anywhere.

My favourite mark is at **Boundary Road**, at the Walmer end of the seafront, near Kingsdown. Other marks include **Sandown Castle**, **Deal Castle**, **Walmer Castle** and the **Kingsdown Butts**. Deal has a pier, built in 1952. It is a stilted pier built over chalk rock and sand which offers excellent fishing for codling and pouting during winter and pouting, pollack, flatfish and the occasional bass and smoothhounds in spring. Fishing is best from the lower deck, and the west corner is best during a flood-tide. Try the east corner when the ebb is running.

Top baits are yellowtail lugworm and peeler crab with ragworm

Kingsdown Butts, near Deal, can produce some superb double-figure cod, like this prime winter fish

for the pollack and fish strip for garfish and scad. Mackerel and garfish can be caught from the pier during sunny August to October days and the same conditions yield a few mullet to bread flake fished between the pier piles.

Kingsdown and **St Margarets Bay** are marks where rock anglers search for bass, cod and occasionally big conger eels. **Kingsdown Butts**, as its name suggests, is an army rifle range. Fishing is available when the Butts are not in use, with fishing from the cliff protection aprons. Essentially a venue of the autumn and winter, although not known nationally because of its constant use by the Army, local anglers spot that firing has ceased and take the opportunity to fish. Cod to 30 lb have been caught from the Butts and in recent years a best conger of 52 lb was landed in the autumn. Access is via the B2057 off the Dover to Deal road. The Butts fishes best at low water with peeler crab, yellowtail and occasionally a large squid bait being the most productive. Farther along the coast **St Margarets Bay** offers similar conditions, although angling space is limited and not possible in summer when the venue is crowded with holidaymakers.

The large harbour complex at **Dover** offers a limited amount of fishing despite its size and, in recent years, the closure of the **Admiralty Pier** because of storm damage has left only the central **Southern Breakwater** and the **Prince of Wales Pier**, in the centre of the harbour, open to anglers. However, there is hope for the Admiralty Pier and the Dover Sea Angling Association are negotiating repairs and hope to re-open the first half of the pier by 1990. The fate of the pier's extension is unknown and it looks as if this excellent bass and cod venue may be lost to angling for good.

By far the major venue at Dover is the **Southern Breakwater**, which is situated in the centre of the outer harbour between the Admiralty Pier and Eastern Arm. The latter is not open for angling. The breakwater is only reachable by boat — return fare £1.50 — which makes the journey to the wall daily from the Dump Head jetty at Wellington Docks. Boats leave from 8 a.m. daily and return at 3.30 p.m. A ticket for the Breakwater is required and these cost 75p, available from the Prince of Wales Pier ticket office.

The Breakwater includes 213 permanent fishing pegs on the central wall plus additional angling from the inside walls at each end. The pegged section offers fishing into the harbour and out to sea, where a large variety of fish can be caught. The outside wall is scoured by very strong flood and ebb tides, which can only be fished by using 6 oz fixed wire sinkers. A midday high-water is

Fish from Dover Breakwater and you too could catch mullet like this.
The best of the bunch weighs 5 lb

the best choice for a visit to the wall, although it is wise not to travel to Dover if the shipping forecast gives a wind strength above Force 5 as this stops the boats ferrying anglers out to the breakwater. Information on boats from the Dover Motor Boat Company (0304 206809). Local tackle shops stock the necessary fixed spiked leads needed to hold bottom here.

Just about every species is at sometime or another caught from the Breakwater. From September through until March cod and codling are plentiful from the outside wall with fish in double figures common. Top baits are yellowtail lugworm, squid and peeler crab. The hotspot for cod is the **Knuckle** (Peg numbers 1 to 13). In the New Year codling move into the harbour and can be caught from the inside wall on all baits. Bass patrol the wall in summer and the new British record bass of 19 lb 0½ oz fell to a whole squid fished down the wall during a flood tide. Also favoured as bait for bass is a whole mackerel head fished alongside the wall when the tide runs west to east. The rising tide switches direction regularly and it pays to check which way the tide is running before casting out.

During spring smoothhounds are regularly caught from the outside wall with fish to 10 lb preferring fresh peeler crab or ragworm. The inside wall offers lots of flatfish with a large head of flounders and dabs all-year-around. These patrol the harbour and are joined by plaice and sole between May and November. Lugworm and small ragworm baits are the most deadly for the flatfish, which can be caught at very short range, with a 30-yard 'plop' all that's necessary. High peg numbers are best for flatfish. Other species include the ever present pouting, which is a pest in summer, when pollack, bass, dogfish or plaice are sought. Mackerel shoal off the outside wall from June onwards as do grey mullet, which can be attracted by dangling a net bag full of bread just under the surface.

The **Prince of Wales Pier** inside the harbour is open daily – tickets are 75p. It is an ideal venue for juniors and disabled anglers because of the easy access. Fishing is good in autumn with whiting, codling, pollack, pouting, dabs, flounders, plaice and mullet plentiful. Top baits include lugworm, ragworm and harbour ragworm, which are particularly deadly for the pollack and flounders when fished alongside the pier wall on a French boom rig.

There is limited beach fishing at Dover with a small section of beach inside the harbour open to angling. Fishing is not allowed from the promenade inside the harbour. To the west of the harbour is **Shakespeare Beach**, which is an excellent venue for cod in winter and bass in summer, although it is often only fished by local anglers.

The stretch of coastline below the **White Cliffs of Dover** and between **Dover** and **Folkestone** is known as **The Warren** and offers seven miles of shore angling from promenade and cliff protection aprons. Access is only possible by foot and therefore this large area is relatively unfished by all but local anglers. Bass, cod, pouting and eels are the main species whilst the area also offers plentiful bait supplies, including peeler crab in summer and lugworm, which can only be dug over the spring tides. Access to the Warren is easiest from the Folkestone end at Wear Bay Road.

Folkestone offers mixed fishing, with the **East Cliff** and Warren area, to the east, best known for bass and eels in spring and summer, while the **Harbour Pier** produces cod and whiting in winter and pouting, pollack, mackerel, mullet, sole, dabs and the odd big conger eel in summer and autumn. The bend of the pier is particularly favoured for dabs and plaice and is best fished at high tide. Tides are fairly strong and a fixed lead is required during spring high water. Angling from Folkestone pier is controlled by the local Folkestone SAC and tickets to fish cost £1, obtainable from local tackle shops. The pier is open from 9 a.m. most days, except during storms.

To the west of Folkestone pier stretches the **Rotunda Beach** and from here, until you get to **Seabrook**, the bottom is all rocks and heavy weed. This is the venue for the angler who prefers to fish with one hook and a big bait for cod, bass and conger. The conger are not plentiful, but nevertheless the venue has a best of 48 lb caught by my father, Charlie Yates. A big fillet of fresh mackerel fished on a calm moonlit night is the way if you have the patience. Try the middle toll gate for that big eel.

Bass are present from June until November, whilst the cod arrive in September and stay until March. The autumn overlap of the two species offers terrific sport and best results are obtained in darkness during the rising tide with peeler crab the top bait. Squid, fresh mackerel and lugworm also find success on occasions. Favourite venues include behind the **Mermaid Café**, **Sandgate Riviera**, **Sandgate Castle** and **Brewers Hill**, although they are not for the angler who fishes with light line or doesn't like losing a few leads.

At Seabrook the coast road actually runs parallel with the sea at **Princes Parade**. This stretch of promenade is perhaps Kent's favourite venue, with anglers able to fish from their parked cars for codling, cod, whiting, dabs, pouting and flounders. Fish are found at 80 yards plus and the venue does favour long-casting. The west end of the Princes Parade fishes best in the storms, whilst the deeper east end is best when the sea is flat. Darkness or following a storm is the best time to fish and keeping an eye on the weather during winter can result in some big catches of cod. Look for a south-westerly during spring tides.

Top baits include: black, common and yellowtail lugworm, snake white ragworm and shellfish such as razorfish. The complete length of Princes Parade contains 200 permanent pegs, spaced at five-yard intervals. These are used by the many clubs who hold competitions on the venue during the winter months. Summer sport from Princes Parade is limited to small pouting and flatfish with mackerel during calm, warm evenings.

Hythe's Marine Parade offers very similar results to Seabrook's Princes Parade, although at Hythe a broader and more sheltered beach offers comfort for the angler during the biggest storms. After a strong south-westerly gale or storm shellfish are washed up the beach as the tide starts to come in − look in the western end of the groynes. Top spots include behind **Hythe swimming pool** and **Yacht Club**, **Ocean Eleven** and close to **Fishermen's Beach**, where the local fishermen keep their boats.

Hythe fishes best during October to March with January excellent in some years for codling and flounders. At the end of the Fishermen's Beach, **Hythe Army Ranges** begins. This stretch of Ministry of Defence beach is open to angling when the Army is not firing. Notices showing firing times are posted at both ends of the range. The Ranges stretch for two miles to Hythe **Redoubt Corner**, which offers excellent cod and codling fishing in the winter. During summer silver eels, pouting, sole, dabs and the odd smoothhound are taken, with the best results at night. Black lug can be dug during long spring tides throughout the range to **Dymchurch** and during the spring tides shellfish can be collected from the sand bars.

The stretch of shoreline from Dymchurch through to **Dungeness** is very shallow and whilst the area is excellent for digging black lugworm and razorfish it offers comparatively poor fishing. Shore results are limited to eels and pouting at the **Willop Sluice**, **Littlestone** and **Greatstone** with an outside chance of bass, smoothhound, sole or plaice in summer and whiting and the odd big cod in winter.

Best results come at night in perfect, flat, calm seas bathed in moonlight, when the big cod come inshore chasing the whiting. Top mark is the **Martello Tower**, near the Sands Estate. During early spring an onshore wind at Littlestone can stir the bass into

Dungeness at its very best. Cod to 17 lb for an angler prepared to fish at night

action during daylight and I have taken some excellent catches of bass to 7 lb on peeler crab. I hasten to add that results are not always guaranteed and fishing Littlestone is hit or miss.

During the 1950s **Dungeness** was the shore angler's Mecca for cod. Some outstanding catches of cod were made from this shingle outcrop, which is ever growing as the Channel current and winds continuously build the 'Point'. The end of this promontory is the cod hotspot, because as the tide sweeps around the 'Point' it creates a small tidal eddy nicknamed the '**Dustbin**'. Line up the two lighthouses to fish the hotspot, but be warned, so many anglers have done the same thing over recent years that the bottom is a nightmare maze of tackle-snagging lost end gear.

Dungeness now hosts two power stations and these pump warm water into the sea. Large bass used to be caught in numbers around the outfalls, but now sport is limited to school bass, which fall for artificial sandeels. The warm water does attract eels, sole and bass late into winter. Peak fishing time is during winter, when the promise of cod attracts thousands of anglers. The crowds make Dungeness difficult to fish at weekends and a novice can quickly spoil a lot of anglers' sport because strong tides can sweep tackle along the beach. Casting distance and the ability to hold bottom is the key to finding the Dungeness cod shoals. Dungeness is reached via the B275, which turns off the A259 at New Romney.

Dengemarsh is a continuation of Dungeness situated to the west of the power station. To reach Dengemarsh, and nearby **Galloways**, you take Robin Hood Lane out of Lydd. The road deteriorates into a pot-holed track for one mile before you reach the beach. It is an ideal venue to turn to when Dungeness is swept by a south-westerly gale over a spring tide because it offers less tide and weed and is fishable when Dungeness is not.

The beach has one other claim to fame − it's the premier sole beach in the South-East. A night tide in July or August can find the soles feeding well, with a dozen fish a tide possible. My best score over the years was 48, using two rods. I always prefer to fish overnight to a dawn high tide and my favourite sole mark is 200 yards east of the end of the road at the mark called the '**Diamond**'.

Black lugworm or small king ragworm are the top baits with lightweight plastic boom rigs a local favourite. Soles can be found very close to the shoreline at Dengemarsh, so it often pays to fish with two rods, one cast long and one fished short. At other times in the summer it produces eels, bass, pouting, dabs, mackerel and plaice, with cod, whiting and flounders possible in winter.

Boat gear for the Kent coast

THERE'S a high proportion of 'owner skippers' living in Kent and dinghy angling, in particular, is popular along the North Kent coast, where there's comparatively safe inshore fishing for all types of fish. Herne Bay hosts the annual National Dinghy Festival held during May, when 300 plus small craft compete in the country's largest dinghy competition.

Along the South Kent coast, charter boats are more prolific, with Ramsgate, Deal, Dover, Folkestone and Dungeness the main centres of boat angling. Here large well-equipped boats fish the English Channel and its many wrecks and sand banks. Many skippers are well known for their wreck and fish-finding skills and boat prices usually reflect results.

Two specific types of boat angling take place around the Kent coast. Much of the charter boat fishing involves the use of chrome or coloured plastic pirks and coloured or white feathers worked over the many Channel sand banks and wrecks for cod. The other type of fishing involves fishing a static bait on the seabed. There are several other variations, including bass and pollack spinning with artificial sandeels, wreck fishing for conger, estuary dinghy fishing and uptide fishing in the shallower waters.

Pirking is considered unsporting by some anglers, although it cannot be denied that it is a very efficient way to catch fish, and, after all, a hectic day's fishing over a wreck with pirk and feathers is exciting. The unsporting side comes from the fact that using heavy metal pirks and feathers, fished 'sink and draw', foulhooks lots of fish, but the technique can be successful and a comparatively novice angler will catch cod.

Top venues in Kent for this method of fishing are Dover, Dungeness and Folkestone, although some skippers at these venues won't allow anglers to use pirks on their boats and much prefer anglers to use large 210 mm artificial sandeels, with black being particularly effective. Check with skippers when booking.

Tackle required for feathering or pirking over a wreck includes a 30 lb class rod, with some anglers preferring to use up to 50 lb class outfits for multi-hook rigs. It is not unknown for three double-figure cod to be hooked at once! Similarly, choose a decent-sized multiplier, 1/0 to 3/0 size being preferable, although choosing a reel is difficult as there is not a standard range of reel sizes. The Penn system of 1/0, 2/0 and so on is used by several other manufacturers. A few models ideal for wreck fishing – they should be filled with 25 lb line for conger or cod – are the ABU Ambassadeur

Nine and Ten, Shimano TLD 10 and TLD 15 and the Daiwa Sealine 250H, 300H and 400H. A butt pad completes the outfit.

For general bottom fishing from charter boats and dinghies choose a 30 lb class rod, while much lighter blanks may be preferred for inshore fishing for bass and flatfish. Reels such as the ABU 7000 are ideal, although again other manufacturers such as Shakespeare, Daiwa, Shimano, Mitchell and Penn offer models of equal dimensions and I only use the ABU as a yardstick. The more sporting angler also may consider using this outfit for wreck fishing using a single feather or 210 mm artificial eel fished on a long, flowing trace.

Two basic rigs work well from the boats working the English Channel. For cod and other big species a six-foot flowing trace is ideal and for single bait fishing for big fish look no further than a Pennel rig. For summer tope, conger or spurdog add a short 12-inch wire bite trace − 60 lb plastic-covered wire − just above the hook. For the smaller species, especially whiting, dabs, and plaice, etc, use a stainless steel three-boom spreader or combination of French-type booms. Leads required to hold bottom vary from 1½ lb for fishing the deepest Channel marks to 8 oz and up to 1 lb maximum for coping with the North Kent coast and most inshore ground.

Uptide casting techniques find considerable success along the North Kent coast and in the shallow waters off Folkestone, Dover and Dymchurch, although it is not generally so successful when used from a small dinghy. Rods of up to 10 feet long are employed with the best being built along beach rod lines. The smaller shore fishing multiplier reels filled with light lines of around 15 lb help to get maximum casting range and beat the tides. A simple one-hook nylon paternoster with bait clip and fixed grip lead completes the outfit, which is especially effective for cod during the winter months.

Top boat baits include all of the sea angling favourites such as lugworm, squid and fish strip. Results, though, do reflect the season. During spring and summer, marks along the North Kent coast respond to fresh peeler crab, which is available locally. Bass, eels, flounders and thornback are taken in good numbers as well. In late summer the bass and rays respond to fish baits, whilst in winter lugworm is the top bait for cod, dabs and whiting, with the yellowtail variety, dug at Sandwich Bay, superior to the common lugworm. Throughout the South Kent coast lugworm and squid cocktails are the winter's favourite bait with yellowtail lugworm tipped with squid being a firm favourite.

One word about squid − the locally caught cuttlefish or large squid seem to work much better than the smaller imported *calimari* squid. Fresh or frozen squid both work well, but make sure you remove the pink skin and look for clean white flesh — a pink tone means that the squid has been in and out of the freezer several times. In summer, fresh mackerel, sandeel, lugworm and ragworm all take fish, with the former particularly successful around the wrecks and offshore rough ground, where species like conger eels, tope, bull huss, spurdog and rays feed. It is always worth taking a spare rod rigged with mackerel feathers to catch bait in summer as fresh, bloody mackerel is second to none as a bait for the bigger species.

Finally, the seas off Dover and Folkestone are some of the busiest in the world and boat anglers should always be aware of the constant threat of collision. Dinghies should carry all the necessary safety equipment, including flares. It is also advisable to use a quick-release buoy on the anchor rope — just in case you have to leave a mark in a hurry.

Boat angling guide to the Kent coast

CHARTER boat fishing is limited along the North Kent coast, with only a few boats operating from **Gravesend**, the **Medway** estuary and **Whitstable**. However, the area offers miles of calm and safe inshore water for dinghy angling, especially around the **Isle of Sheppey** and **Herne Bay**. In fact, Herne Bay is considered the centre of dinghy fishing in the county because it has excellent launching facilities, including the **Neptune Jetty** situated to the east of the pier. Other slipways in the vicinity include those near **Hampton Jetty** and **Whitstable** harbour.

During spring, dinghy catches include eels, flounders, bass, smoothhounds and thornback ray with the inshore sandbanks within five miles offering the best of the sport. Later in the summer the bigger bass are caught from the **Pan Sands** and **Margate Sands**, with fish of 10 lb common in some years. Feathers, Red Gills and pirks all take their share of fish. At the end of the summer and into autumn the bigger bass fall to large mackerel and squid baits fished on flowing trace close to the seabed.

The most famous of the bass marks off Herne Bay is the Pan Sands, which holds the current British best for bass at 19 lb 9 oz 2 drms. The **Pan Sands inner bank** fishes best during the first hour of the flood tide and during the last two hours of the ebb tide. Another favourite mark is the **Woolpack Sandbank** some three miles off Reculver's twin towers. The bank is an excellent dinghy mark for thornback and bass in the warmer months.

Inshore fishing for flounders is excellent from marks off **Hampton Jetty, Herne Bay Pier** and **Reculver**, whilst the long shingle bank off **Whitstable** called the Street offers bass, flounders and eels for dinghy anglers fishing in less than six feet of water on the tide side of the bank. During winter cod, whiting and dabs are taken by the dinghies with the **North-West shingles** the top mark.

Dinghy fishing between **Minnis Bay** and **Margate** includes inshore fishing from the Pan Sands and Margate Sands for bass, smoothhounds and thornback in summer, with winter cod inshore to the south-east of **Margate**, off the **Thanet** chalk ledges and from marks off the **North Foreland**. The inshore reefs around Margate hold bass, which take spinners during June and July. Try trolling an artificial eel 150 metres behind a slow-moving dinghy, although calm, clear conditions are of paramount importance for this method to work. Slipways are situated at **Minnis Bay** and at the bottom of **Beach Avenue**, Birchington.

A large and well-equipped charter fleet operates out of **Ramsgate** harbour with boats not restricted by the tide except during very low springs. Boats find fish all year with cod inshore from the North Foreland marks throughout the winter months and during spring. In summer the main venue is the **Goodwin Sands**, with its many wrecks and sandbars holding thornback ray, tope, bass, plaice, smoothhound and dogfish. The inshore area of the **Stour Estuary** in **Pegwell** and **Sandwich Bays** holds flatfish for much of the year, with some good catches of plaice recorded in spring and summer. Limited launching facilities are available at **Ramsgate** harbour and at the **Eastern Undercliff**.

Deal, and nearby **Walmer**, are both home to a large charter fleet or craft launched from the beach. Positioned in the lee of the prevailing south-westerly winds, boats in the area are very seldom prevented from going to sea, although beach launching can be difficult in a strong south-westerly swell. Excellent fishing is enjoyed during the winter, especially with cod. Marks are within two miles of the shore, whilst during the summer months the **Goodwin Sands** are easily reached. Fish the Goodwins during an ebb tide run-off with a flowing trace and hook baited with fish to attract tope, thornback, dogfish and bass. Winter cod respond best to yellowtail lugworm and large squid baits, also fished on a flowing trace.

To the west of Deal, marks off **Kingsdown** and **Fan Bay**, near Dover, are known for their good cod and plaice fishing within one mile of the shore. There are a considerable number of wrecks

A 30 lb cod caught by Mark Weatherly out of Folkestone aboard the charter boat *Dorothy*

within easy reach of the **Deal** and **Walmer** boats, and hauls consist of cod, conger and pollack with feathers, pirks and artificial eels all scoring well, especially for the cod. Dinghy anglers should head for the Kingsdown SAC, where there's excellent launching facilities close to the **Zetland Arms at Kingsdown**. Inshore dinghy fishing under the **White Cliffs of Dover** is excellent for cod in winter and bass and plaice in summer.

Despite its large harbour, **Dover** has only a small charter fleet of 12 or so craft. These offer inshore fishing for cod and plaice in season, although several of the boats specialise in offshore wreck and sandbank fishing. The **Varne Bank**, some ten miles out, is first choice for pirking for cod with feathers and Red Gills fished sink and draw scoring well during most of the year. Inshore fishing is best during winter for cod, with fish to 20 lb plus common from marks at **Fan Bay** and **Warren Bay**, especially during October and November. A six-foot flowing trace is the best rig for bottom fishing and yellowtail lugworm, dug fresh from nearby Sandwich Bay, the top bait. The bigger winter cod are taken on whole squid fished on a two-hook Pennel rig.

Strong tides are encountered throughout the region and upwards of 1 lb of lead is needed to hold bottom, especially during the spring flood tide. Uptide casting is possible in the relatively shallow Fan Bay area, to the east of Dover Harbour, and light line sportsmen take some excellent catches of cod during the winter on simple one-hook paternoster rigs and fixed grip leads fished uptide. The Dover fleet is not restricted by the tide, except during the spring lows. Boats can continue fishing inside the harbour during winter gales, although results are limited.

Folkestone's charter fleet fluctuates from year to year according to business. It is therefore wise to stick with a reputable and regular skipper. Boats specialising in fishing the **Varne Bank, The Ridge** and the many wrecks in the area are famed for their marvellous cod catches. Fishing the Varne Bank is particularly productive for cod during summer and autumn with pirks. Red Gills and large cod feathers are responsible for huge catches.

The basic set-up is a 12 oz plus pirk below three white feathers or artificial eels, which should be black. The rig is fished sink and draw over the sandbanks as the boat drifts over the peaks and troughs below the waves. Sport is hectic when a shoal of cod is located and three fish of 10 lb apiece on one drop is not uncommon. As the drift continues, sport tails off in the deeper water, although large mackerel, gurnards and some big bass are included in catches. The Varne is also famed for its turbot and a few boats fish at anchor during the summer to take these giant flatfish, plus

Dinghy anglers prepare to launch at Foreness, a sheltered mark that offers good mixed fishing

bass, cod and tope. Farther out in the English Channel is another sandbank, **The Ridge**, which is equally productive.

Throughout the region there are several hundred wrecks, including lots of war-time hulks. Many of these have been 'topped and tailed' with explosives in recent years to remove projecting areas which were a hazard to shipping. This has spread wreckage over a larger area to form fish-holding reefs and many top Folkestone skippers can pinpoint these 'fishy' hotspots.

The inshore fishing from smaller boats and dinghies has declined in recent years, although sport during autumn and winter for cod is excellent. Top inshore marks include the **Rough Ground**, close to the pilot buoys four miles off Folkestone and Sandgate, and inshore marks off the **Warren** and **Metropole rocks**. Other marks include 'holes', which show up on charts of the area, including one off Folkestone Pier and another in the Warren. These are particularly favoured for conger in summer and big cod in winter.

Launching facilities for dinghies are available at **Folkestone** harbour. Slipways are also situated at **Sandgate**, behind the Folkestone Rowing Club, at **Seapoint, Seabrook** and at **Twiss Road, Hythe**. All of these slipways are subject to beach movement, which can make landing and launching at high water difficult.

Sandgate, Seabrook, Hythe and **Dymchurch** are all areas fished mainly by dinghies, although Folkestone charter boats do venture into the area and there are a limited number of small beach-launched charter boats at Hythe. Fishing is mainly inshore for flatfish and bass in summer and cod in winter. The area off **Hythe Ranges**, between Hythe and Dymchurch, is out of bounds when the Army firing range is in use. Beach launching is available as previously mentioned, with additional slipways at Dymchurch, although launching is tricky because the tide recedes some 200 yards. Marks particularly favoured include the **Mulberry Harbours** off Greatstone, where some excellent bass catches have been made.

Charter boats fishing from **Dungeness**, where boats are launched from the beach, are limited. Fishing for cod, conger, pollack and ling takes place over the many war-time wrecks, which are famed for their big fish. Feathers and pirks score well, as does fish bait for conger. Dungeness did, in fact, hold the British conger record for many years and there may still be a record-breaker hiding away in a wreck.

During summer good results are likely over the inshore marks in **Rye Bay**, where there is some excellent sport with flatfish, especially plaice. Top baits are lugworm on both flowing trace or spreader rigs. In winter Dungeness is equally famed for its cod fishing afloat as it is for its shore fishing. Fish to 30 lb plus are regularly hooked within two miles of the shore. As with most other parts of the Kent coast, tides are strong and leads of around 1 lb are needed to hold a bait on the bottom.

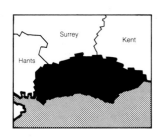

John Darling

SUSSEX

JOHN DARLING, the Seaford-based angler, journalist
and photographer, tells how to be a successful
angler along the Sussex shoreline.

THE CRADLE OF SEA ANGLING

SEA fishing has always been good along the coast of 'Sussex by the Sea'. It's one of the places where the sport was first developed. The county has six sheltered harbours; Rye, Newhaven, Brighton, Shoreham, Littlehampton and Chichester, and numerous steep shingle beaches from which hundreds of boats put to sea. A new marina is currently being built at Eastbourne.

This part of England, bordering the Channel, is known as the affluent South-East, and this is reflected in the facilities to be found here. Most of the coastal towns have professionally run tackle shops that offer a wide range of modern equipment, together with fresh bait.

Deep-water anglers have a wide choice of charter boats based at most of the main harbours, and some of the skippers are well known for the regularity with which they produce large bags of fish.

The shore angler has plenty of choice, too. There are sheltered harbours, marinas, fast-flowing estuaries, sandflats, steep shingle beaches, fissured reefs, huge chalk cliffs, little bays, piers, breakwaters and promenades – and they all produce good fish at some time or another.

Anglers who trail decent-size boats are poorly catered for, however. There's a good public slipway at Rye, but nothing suitable westwards until Newhaven marina, where access is limited. There is one upriver at Ropetackle quay, Shoreham, but this is tidal, and there are access points for easily managed boats at Littlehampton, but no more decent slipways between here and Chichester harbour, where there are ramps at Cobnor and Dell Quay.

Tides around this coast are two and three-quarter hours in advance of the times given for London Bridge. This is accurate enough considering that the tide turns earlier inshore than out deep, turns later in the upper reaches of Sussex's long, narrow estuaries, and that the tides themselves don't always stick to their predicted times. The flow is eastwards, and the ebb runs westwards.

The currents flow in a regular pattern. With a range of about seven metres on springs, they're powerful around estuaries and headlands, but moderate along most of the shoreline. They run strongly offshore, and a 2 lb lead on 40 lb nylon line is sometimes insufficient to anchor a big bait alongside a deep-water wreck.

Sussex is one of the warmest and windiest places in England. Summer days can be especially hot and balmy, when high pressure drifts over from the Continent, bringing warm breezes from the land rather than the chill air off the Atlantic. The sea temperature is one of the highest around Britain, and this favours migrating fish.

Our bad weather comes straight in off the Atlantic, although its not unusual for thunderstorms and other nasties to drift up from the Bay of Biscay. In winter, the worst weather comes off the Continent, but this time from Siberia — bitter east winds, loaded with snow. This can happen any time in January or February, although heavy snow is rare. From then on, it can pour with rain at any time, but the sun shines a lot from April onwards.

Windy weather, with the rest of the country experiencing pouring rain, can be hot and bright on summer days along this coast. The South Downs are the first cloud-forming obstruction the air meets for a couple of thousand miles, but the wind carries the clouds away from the coast. June is a consistently warm month, July can be either perfect or appalling, while August can be very windy. November and December are generally warm.

Winter sea conditions can be calm for days on end when the continental high pressure is shielding us from fronts coming in off the Atlantic. This generally leads to severe gales in the West Country. Midsummer days can be as perfect as anywhere else on Earth, the sea flat, blue, crystal clear, and gently whispering along the shoreline.

To this coast come cod in winter, although the shore fishing for them isn't very special anywhere west of Newhaven. The main run is October to early January. In March the fish move to deep-water wrecks and reefs.

Summer wreck catches, generally 30 or so miles from land, often exceed a ton of fish per day. The wreck fishing generally is excellent for big cod and conger, large ling and medium pollack. Beyond a few sand and shingle banks, reefs and ledges, the seabed off Sussex is somewhat flat. However, human folly and wars have added many fish-holding features.

Plaice move in to spawn over hard rock ground early in March, then move inshore, especially to reefy ground, as the summer progresses. They are frequently caught by specialist anglers. Soles are abundant from early summer onwards, and large ones are caught through to Christmas.

Mullet are abundant — thick-lipped around piers and in the harbours, thin-lipped up the estuaries, and golden-greys from

Lancing beach — and several others in settled weather.

Bass turn up everywhere. This coast is on the map for fish migrating up from Biscay and from west of the Isle of Wight, and these supplement our resident stock. Large schools have been seen harrying baitfish several miles from land the entire length of the coast.

Some of these fish take up residence around inshore reefs during the summer, and use these vantage points for sorties along the beaches, up estuaries, around piers and so on. They can turn up anywhere.

Tope fishing is generally good from boats, and sometimes a wrecking party comes home with a shark — usually a porbeagle. Spurdogs are often abundant early in the summer, but dogfish can be a nuisance — lesser spotteds and small bull huss offshore, small spurdogs along some beaches. There is a run of smoothhounds offshore in summer, but nobody fishes crab bait out that deep, and few are caught.

The big skate that once made Hastings famous have long since gone, and few rays are caught along these beaches. Sometimes a stingray is caught at Littlehampton or Wittering, but generally the only rays are much too small to keep. Some good thornbacks can be caught out deep — but they aren't numerous.

Large shoals of mackerel throng deeper water marks along the shore when the tides and weather are right during June and July, but in August they can be hard to find — even offshore. Garfish and scad are sometimes abundant in settled weather. Herrings are frequently feathered up off Newhaven Arm in autumn. Sprats are abundant offshore, and so are sandeels at times. Many of these fish make good bait for large congers from piers and rocky shores.

Black bream catches are famous from the Kingmere rocks off Littlehampton, and sometimes small ones are caught from the open beach. Other shore fish include whiting and pouting throughout the year, and flounders, which are excellent in January, when they migrate down the rivers and along the coast before spawning.

Tackle and techniques for shore fishing

THE varied nature of the Sussex shoreline allows fish to be caught by many different techniques, using a range of tackle. In summer, a lightweight bass rod, a medium-power beachcaster, a spinning

Author of your guide to Sussex, John Darling, with the spoils of a night's cod fishing

rod, a fly rod, a freshwater float rod, and a 30 lb class boat rod for conger fishing from piers and jetties. In autumn and winter, a medium beachcaster, and a pair of long-distance casting rods will cover all eventualities.

This is quite some armoury, but it enables you to take advantage of the many opportunities that exist along the shoreline. The light bass rod is ideal for fishing the rocks and surfy bays. The medium-power rod is a great all-rounder for general beach fishing, and the pair of long-distance rods are what most people prefer for codding off the beach.

During the summer months, the light bass rod can be used for float fishing around piers and jetties, while the spinning and fly rods are fun when the school bass, mackerel, garfish, sea trout, small pollack and scad are feeding.

The freshwater float rod is useful for catching garfish, mackerel and small pollack around the piers, and for the numerous mullet that inhabit the harbours and estuaries.

Reels could be any of the top-of-the-range models currently available on the market — they're built for the job and are unlikely to cause trouble during use. Small multipliers are ideal for casting, although a more powerful reel is required for hauling in conger.

Small fixed-spool reels make life easy when spinning and mullet fishing, although a centre-pin trotting reel is valuable in some of the mullet swims. Fly fishermen would be wise to consider one of the new generation of moulded carbon-fibre reels as they are impervious to salt.

Lines for sea fishing off Sussex should always be of nylon monofilament. Various breaking strains are used around here. For open beach work, 10–16 lb monofilament is preferred because few of the beaches have any serious snags fouling them. This gauge of line is also suitable for light boat fishing. However, around Fairlight, to the east of Hastings, and between Eastbourne and Brighton, extensive reefs are to be found beneath the cliffs.

Big bass come to these reefs in midsummer and autumn, but the terrain is so rough that heavier lines are required. Much of the rock has sharp flints embedded in it, and these swiftly shred light lines. Something around 23–35 lb is suitable, but with 12 lb links to the weight and hook. For spinning and float fishing for mackerel or mullet, lines of around 4–8 lb test are preferred.

Various designs of terminal tackle have been developed along this coast, and have stood the test of time. The best rigs are always the simplest, requiring the minimum of knots and hardware to arouse the fish's suspicions. However, the design of a paternoster for long-distance casting also needs to be streamlined for casting.

Figure 4 Bass rock paternoster tackle

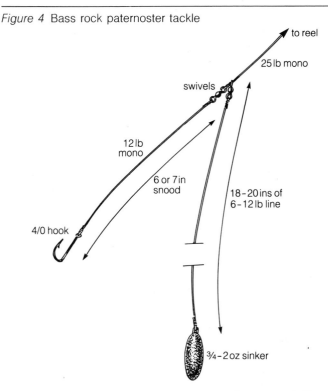

to reel

25 lb mono

swivels

12 lb
mono

6 or 7 in
snood

18-20 ins of
6-12 lb line

4/0 hook

¾-2 oz sinker

The easy way to make this is to take a Paul Kerry rotating swivel and tie it to the end of your casting leader. Tie a yard of this leader to the opposite side, slide on a bait-clip, and tie on a lead-clip. The hook-link rarely needs to be more than a couple of feet long, and a seven-inch link prevents tangles in a rough sea.

Because there are few places where the tidal currents run strong, the most popular design of weight is the long-tailed Breakaway design, either with beads or an elastic band. Many of the beaches give on to flat rock or open sand, and this design of sinker, in either 4 or 5 oz, will suffice for much beach work. However, where the tide is negligble, plain leads without wires are to be recommended.

Sometimes it is advisable to have two hooks on the end of the trace, particularly when fishing for cod. The trick is to tie in an extra piece of line with a four-turn water knot, about six inches or so from the end of the trace. This rig is called a 'wishbone' and it can be adapted in various ways.

One way is to have one very short trace and a six-inch one, so that a long bait has a hook at each end. Another way is to have one side four inches, the other six inches long and bait the short side. If a whiting or small pouting takes this bait, it can be left tethered out there as a livebait. The other hook is for any hungry predator that grabs the livebait.

A trick much used by matchmen is to make both lengths of the 'wishbone' the same, so that they can be clipped to the same bait-clip. Both traces are loaded with white or small red ragworm. Some of these may fly off on the journey out to sea, but when the hooks reach the bottom, enough remains to make an attractive spread on the seabed.

Some of the bassy reefs and surfy bays are best fished with really light tackle, using a 2 oz bomb on a running paternoster. This is simple to make, provided you remember to tie the weight to the swivel that slides along the line.

Take two small swivels – they must be unobtrusive, but not so small that the eye of the sliding swivel jams on the knot to the fixed swivel. Slide one on to the reel line, and tie the other to the end. Tie 18 inches of 12 lb line to the running swivel, and fix a small bomb to the other end. Tie nine inches of 12 lb line to the other end of the fixed swivel, and end it with a 4/0 fine wire hook.

This tackle is used for casting large baits of soft crab, squid and mackerel as far as possible – generally no more than 70 yards at best. But this is often much too far – bass are happy to feed in knee-deep water.

Along much of this coast, the best fishing for bass in surf or from reefs is on the early flood tide. As soon as there's a bit of push in the water, the bass come close to the edge to see what titbits will be revealed – just as we watch the tide go down, to see what will be uncovered.

Consequently, this rig can be slimmed down even more for reef fishing, where the strength of the mainline needs to be beefed up, to cope with the flints. A sinker as light as 3/4 oz can be cast quite hard when tied to the sliding swivel with 6 lb line. Alternatively, an old spark plug, with the gap tapped shut against a rock, makes an expendable alternative for closerange fishing.

This rig works by allowing a fish to mouth the bait warily for some time. It can pick up the bait and drop it, take line off the reel, and generally mess about without feeling the rod-tip or the tension on the line. The secret is the short trace – it emphasises the bass's first reaction to the bait, warning the angler to look sharp and give the fish no cause for alarm until it's too late.

One rig that produces deadly results is the slide-down rig. The principle is that a stop is tied on the line and, after the sinker has been cast out, the bait slides down to the stop. It is used for

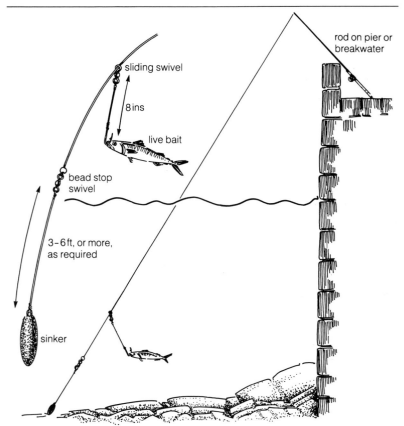

Figure 5 Slide-down rig

fishing livebaits — or where large baits are required to be suspended above the bottom. It is almost always used from piers.

The easy way to go about making this rig is to tie a swivel to the mainline, and a few feet of line to the lead — this line can be quite weak in snaggy areas because the rig won't work too well when cast far out. Its efficiency depends on the line entering the sea at quite a steep angle, otherwise the bait gets lost half-way.

Above the swivel fixed to the mainline should be another swivel, but free to slide. Tie your trace to this and fix on a hook. Before lobbing out, catch the hook in one of the rod rings so that the line runs out freely through the swivel. When the sinker has firmly gripped the seabed, affix a small whiting, pouting or strip of mackerel or squid and let the sea take it down to the stop.

In some places, big conger and bass are known to feed. Often this requires a stealthy approach with a large bait on a running leger. This is easy to make, and is really an extension of the two-swivel running paternoster tackle outlined for bass earlier. Stronger line is needed for shore conger: 20–25 lb test.

Have one running swivel, one fixed swivel. You can ensure a really strong join by passing the line through the fixed swivel twice before forming the knot. To the running swivel, tie six inches of line that is strong enough to cast with.

To the fixed swivel tie two feet of spare mainline, and end this with a swivel and a foot of fine steel trace wire of the same breaking strain. Ignore the nylon-covered stuff and go for straight multi-strand wire. Crimp a 5/0 hook to this and load it with fresh mackerel, squid, cuttle or pouting. This is a useful rig for general inshore boat fishing. The steel trace may be omitted if conger are neither wished for nor expected.

Float fishing is popular around the piers in summer. During the day, mullet, small wrasse, school bass, mackerel, garfish, scad and small pollack are to be caught on little strips of mackerel fished in the upper layers of water. The easy way to rig for them is with a small sliding float, setting the depth with a small bead and a stop-knot on the line above the float.

A small drilled bullet or two cocks the float. Casting is easier if these are trapped between two swivels. The trace – about a yard long – provides the bait with movement, letting it be wafted around by the waves and current.

Bait presentation is essential. It must look like a small injured fish. Use a sharp knife to slice a three-inch by half-inch section of silver mackerel or garfish skin, with just enough flesh to keep the skin from collapsing. Hook it twice through one end on a size 6 hook, leaving the bait to dangle enticingly rather than bunch around the bend.

The same rig, but with a beefier rod, reel and terminal tackle, can be used for bass fishing. At dawn and late into the night, float-fished prawns or live peeler crabs will catch fish from the many piers, jetties, bridges and harbour installations where these fish come to browse when the bustle of the day is over.

Many of these predators will take a spinner or small Red Gill fished from the right places at the right times of day. With the shoaling fish, this depends on the tide and weather. They are more dependent on the movements of the baitfish.

The more interesting predators, however, move at dusk and dawn. It is indeed an experience to catch bass and sea trout on one of those magical June nights when it never quite gets dark. The best spinners and Red Gills are blue-silver or green-silver, like the fry, smelts, sprats and sandeels they represent.

Places and ways to use these lures – and plugs – have not been widely developed along this coast, but the opportunities exist, nevertheless. The water close inshore is not calm and clear for long, but feeding bass, sea trout and big mackerel are sometimes encountered unexpectedly during calm conditions. The places where these blitzes are likely to occur are mentioned later – they tend to be provoked by the tides and winds gathering the fry into certain corners and on to specific beaches.

The easiest spinner to use is one with built-in weight, although a single feathered lure, fished on a paternoster, works well. Red Gills can be fished the same way. Plugs, more than other lures, require to be fished carefully over these reefs as their many hooks will readily snag the rocks and weed.

In some sheltered corners, all of the above predators can be caught on fly tackle. This is generally a long-range reservoir rod armed with a slow-sink or floating size 9 shooting head. When rocks and weed are around, a stripping basket on the belt saves line from tangling and keeps it safe for the next cast.

Flies should be hair-wing streamers on size 4–6 hooks, made of pearl Flashabou. Silvery-blue and greenish lures, with a dab of hot orange for the scarlet throat hackle, will catch most sea fish. A 6- to 9-foot leader around 10 lb test enables windknots to be quickly unravelled.

School bass are suckers for flies, so file off the barb and simply shake the fish free while it is in the water. However, in order to save money on useless feathers, here's my advice on how to catch mackerel. Their huge eyes are brilliant at picking up the least flicker from a tiny fry, so they have no problem seeing a size 1 stainless steel hook. So there is no point paying out money for a string of feathers when it is as easy to tie up a series of blood-loops and fix a stainless steel hook to each one. A swivel at the top, a weight clipped to the bottom, and the rig is complete.

Standard techniques are required for the mullet around Sussex. In general, float fishing with fish or bread is effective around piers and in the more industrialised estuaries. Outside these, bread and ragworm are preferred for the thick-lipped and the thin-lipped mullet respectively.

The latter, which inhabit the upper limit of the brackish water, can be taken on small ragworm-baited bar-spoons – like the Mepps and ABU's Droppen. This technique is effective, but not widely used, in Sussex.

One reason that bread is so popular with mullet is that if the bait is set to fish too close to the bottom, the result will be flounders. Dozens are caught during late May and June, when they return from spawning. Light float tackle works for them, too. Instead of the sound of gulls, though, there's the sound of frogs from the marshland drains. Different.

Angling along a 100-mile shoreline

THE A259 coast road starts at Folkestone, meets Sussex at Rye, and hugs the sea for nearly 100 miles before ending at Chichester. Between these two towns the road is rarely much more than a brisk walk from dozens of excellent places to go beach fishing and bait collecting.

A wide variety of fish comes to these shores, brought by the tides and seasons, and by the need to eat and reproduce. It is easy to forget this when confronted by all the towns that rim the sea. There are precious few undeveloped areas between Hastings and Bognor. Even so, there are still times when and places where you can stand feeling the line in a lively surf and experience that delightful sensation of being entirely on your own.

The fish don't feel like this. As their migrations bring them to the shrimp-filled sandflats and the sheltering reefs, they're unaware of all this urbanisation, just as we can barely glimpse what goes on beneath the waves. For this reason it's not essential to walk miles to a remote headland far from the madding crowd. Many excellent marks lie alongside the 'promenade'. So let's drive down the A259 and see where to stop off.

Right on the boundary with Kent lies the sleepy village of **Camber**. The turning is signposted two miles before Rye. Stop by the golf course or drive through the village to the sea wall, and walk back towards Rye Harbour.

On low spring tides this vast expanse of sand dries to reveal some of the biggest black lug in Sussex. It's too shallow for fishing, but the dunes are popular with photographers shooting naked ladies – hence the size of the lug, perhaps!

Drive on to **Rye**, over the River Rother, with its excellent thin-lip mullet upstream at Iden, around the historic town and over the River Tillingham, where the road turns back on itself. Just past the next bend, a turning left takes you over Rye's third river, the Brede, and to Rye Harbour, two miles down.

Fish this estuary at the top or bottom of the tide because the current is fierce. Walk down another mile and fish the mouth of the channel around low water for bass, using crabs gathered from the rocks at Pett or Fairlight. In autumn a few cod get caught during lumpy conditions, and winter flounders are sometimes

It is bass like this which draw shore anglers to the Sussex coastline

abundant, particularly on shellfish baits.

The sands on this side are very shallow. They extend the length of **Winchelsea Beach**, which is signposted about three miles out of Rye. The entire area offers excellent lugworm on all but the shortest tides, but very few people bother to fish here.

However, bass, soles, whiting and cod are caught in abundance by old-timers, who set sand lines. One problem is access, the other is that numerous wooden groynes and sea defences run out to sea and parallel to the shore. These aren't fun to cast over when the fish move inshore at night.

At the far end of the beach road rise the cliffs of **Fairlight**. They're made of clay and sandstone, and are sliding into the sea so fast that the once-long gardens of bijou residences are now mere strips separating the bricks from the brink.

Extensive reefs separated by strips of muddy sand run out to sea from beneath these cliffs. Only those reefs that catch the tide produce fish. The 'mud-holes' rarely offer much for the angler. Low water and early flood produce best results. High tide can be fished from the beach at **Pett** and from cliff ledges at Fairlight. Peeler crab is the bait, and not just for the bass. Silver eels and smoothhounds are caught here, too.

The best months are the warm ones, when soles and conger can be taken by night. Winter fishing has never been widely regarded around this part, although some cod are caught amid the rocks and peat beds at **Pett Level** by people escaping the crowds.

Rejoin the A259 again, and negotiate the long, steep hill that leads into **Hastings**. It's a big hill − 575 feet − and often the road up there is frozen when other parts are clear. It's a point to remember when dashing back from Dungie in the early hours.

Tucked under the brow of the cliff is the delapidated breakwater of what was Hastings harbour. The top of the tide produces bass, soles, plaice and mackerel in summer, while winter tides bring cod, whiting, flounders and dabs.

The pier at Hastings offers the best fishing, both summer and winter. The structure attracts the predators like bass and conger, while mullet, mackerel, small pollack and garfish are to be found in midwater.

The structure protrudes a fair way into the tide, and this gives the shore caster greater access to plaice and soles, and to the cod in winter. Some reasonable bags of cod are caught from October to January. Between the piers, the sands are interspersed with small reefs. Bass visit them, particularly in June and July, although results are better from Fairlight.

At **Bexhill**, the most famous mark is to the west of the clock tower on the seafront, where a gully produces consistent winter cod fishing. During the summer months, this beach yields bass, silver eels, whiting, pouting, plaice, soles, and so on, particularly when the sea is settling after a blow.

Extensive sandflats start at Bexhill, which boasts the most elderly population in Britain, and extend in an uninterrupted sweep to Eastbourne. There's good lugworm digging around this bay, especially on the long spring tides, and storms wash razorfish, mussels and whelks ashore at Cooden.

Cooden Beach, **Norman's Bay** – William the Conquerer landed here in 1066 – and **Pevensey Bay** are all shallow, but the fishing can be excellent, particularly early in the tide, around darkness and dawn. Plaice, bass and eels are caught in summer, cod, whiting, dabs and flounders in winter. Prospecting at low tide shows where the channels and other fish-attracting features lie.

Take the A259 out of Pevensey Bay, and you'll come across a new marina. The impact of this on the fishing has yet to be felt, but as it lies so close to the best deep-water wrecking, charter boats are bound to turn up. Mullet will be there, and maybe fishing will be permitted from the breakwater – if they build one. Certainly the beach at **White Horses**, between the Martello towers, will change. Currently it's a good stretch, and the same angling advice applies as for the rest of the bay.

Langney Point is the place to fish over high tide. The road east from the Leisure Pool roundabout takes you to it. There's a sewer and a concrete wall, which make life tricky. Fish come from both sides, however; good bass are taken after periods of rough seas in summer and cod in winter. Tides run swiftly through this deep-water mark, and a variety of fish are caught here. It's a good place for mackerel when the water is clear in midsummer.

Follow the road along the seafront to **Eastbourne Pier**. Not much fishing takes place amid the wooden breakwaters on each side because the bottom is sandy, producing little of consequence. The pier offers mullet, mackerel, and all the mini-predators in summer, while bass of all sizes sometimes shoal amid the girders.

Float-fished prawns and small pouting work for them, usually early or late in the day. Winter codding can be good, too – this elegant Victorian structure has witnessed many a night when the anglers have loaded up with fish. There's a modest charge – about £1 for a day's fishing, and it shuts at 10 p.m.

Further along is the **Wish Tower**, and the start of the reefs that have made this area famous for bass fishing. The tower itself is now a cafeteria for tourists, but big bass are taken at high tide after dark on crab, while winter tides bring cod.

The rocks become increasingly rugged westwards to **Beachy Head**. A turning off the seafront takes you to marks such as the **Sugar Loaf** and **Holywell Lagoon**. For the marks at **Cow Gap**, **Falling Sands**, **Frenchman's Cove**, and **The Ledge**, park on the bend at the end of the seafront road. The footpath leads past a small tea-bar. It's a fair walk to the steps down to the shore.

There are a couple of dozen marks to fish along here. Each works at a specific state of tide, and you can follow the bass 24 hours a day by walking from mark to mark. The only snag is that they don't keep to the same timetable year in year out. This boulder country is treacherous, though, so don't fish it alone if you're not used to it, particularly at night.

For the bass, fish close in to the rocks with big baits of edible or velvet swimming crab. Ordinary shore crabs are less effective. However, these rocks are full of bait, so there's no problem gathering it between June and August.

Everybody has their own secret marks, but this is probably less important than having the right bait out there when a bass wanders past. The best rock marks are exposed to the tide. However, when the current pushes strongly, the fish move to the edge — almost to your feet.

Low tide and the start of the flood are best. This may be because so much sea life has to retreat with the ebb as it uncovers these reefs. Such a migration would produce a band of crabs and prawns along the low-tide mark, waiting for the flood.

Never be in too much of a hurry to leave a mark and try the next one. Often the biggest bass are last to arrive — the 10-pounders like a fair depth of water over their back.

The Ledge mark used to produce consistently good spring cod fishing in March and April. Some of the other reefs along this stretch also attract the cod in spring. Some are caught each year, but it's not like it was — but may be again, one day.

Back on the A259, drive along Beachy Head and down to the next valley — **East Dean**. Turn left to **Birling Gap**. This sandy bay fishes well in a surf for bass, generally around half-flood. Crab and kipper are the time-tested baits. Cod and whiting frequent this beach in winter, usually at high tide.

The rocks back to **Beachy Head lighthouse** offer good bass and crabbing. Conger, too, can be caught, mainly on fish baits, although sometimes they take crabs intended for bass. Conger fishing is best by night, particularly in surfy seas. However, some of these reef eels are large — 30 lb or more — so powerful tackle is required to winch them clear of the snags.

Pevensey Bay is renowned for its prime flatfish

From Birling Gap to **Cuckmere Haven** is an hour's walk under the **Seven Sisters** cliffs. Half-way along lie the twin reefs of **Crowlink**. They're readily visible at low tide. The nearest point produces bass and conger in summer, cod in winter. Low spring tides are best, and usually the fishing peters away to nothing by half-flood, eliminating the problem of being cut off by the tide.

Take the main road over the Seven Sisters and stop at the **River Cuckmere**. The mullet fishing is good in this river, usually over the low-water period when there's little current.

There are two car parks in this valley from which to strike out to picturesque **Cuckmere Haven**. This shallow shingle beach offers excellent bass fishing, particularly in the river-mouth in surf, and fly fishing is often effective when the water clears. Cod can be caught here from low to high water, although the best place is under **Haven Brow**, the first of the Seven Sisters cliffs.

Here, the low-tide mark comes to the base of the shingle bank and this deep water is attractive to cod in winter. In autumn, cod, bass and conger are caught here. The rocks on each side of the bay are noted for bass fishing in calm weather − they don't like it too rough in this bay.

Seaford seafront faces south-west and receives a buffeting in heavy weather. This long shingle beach didn't exist a few years ago − the shingle was brought here from a bank off Littlehampton to prevent the sea wall from being smashed by big seas.

The long shingle beach extends from the cliffs of **Seaford Head** through to **Newhaven**. It offers good general fishing for the usual local species. The early flood tide and over the top produce most bass. Winter codding is best from half-flood, over the top, and back to half-ebb. The new beach has speeded up the tide, but there are now few features to concentrate the fish.

Close to the cliffs are a sewer and a jetty, both of which produce well. It was here that I started sea fishing. The sewer pipe produces bass from low tide upwards − there's a large reef lying between the pipe and the Martello tower. Cod fishing can be good, starting two hours before high water until shortly before low water. Conger come here too − the ebb tide brings best results by night.

This reef is called **Town Rocks** and lies close to shore. In summer it is depicted by plastic bottles marking crab-pots − sometimes over 100 of them. It is the only feature between here and Newhaven. Some large plaice live in the sand patches amid these reefs.

Rejoin the A259 at the Abbots Lodge Motor Inn and head towards **Newhaven**. After a quarter of a mile, take the first turning left and park near the railway line. Walk through the ruined tide mills (yes, mills driven by the tide), to **Tidemills** beach. This is flat sand, backed by shingle. Some black lug can be dug here. It's better closer to the east pier at Newhaven, but the going is wet and stony.

Cod, whiting, pouting and dabs come here in winter; bass, seatrout, mackerel, garfish, infant thornbacks, golden-grey mullet, gurnard, soles and a variety of others in summer. When the water is flat and clear, swarms of goldengrey mullet can be seen as dark patches as the tide floods up the shingle.

This is an unusual beach − the sand beneath the low-tide mark is flat and featureless, apart from a couple of lumps of concrete. The tide is the attraction. A back eddy flows up the Ouse at Newhaven, and the corridor between this and the main flood eastwards is a noted fishing spot. Obviously this changes between neap and spring tides, and according to the weather.

This beach offers shelter out of the main push of tide, both to big fish and the tiddlers they feed on. Its greatest claim to fame is that the flounder record was once broken here.

In a south-easterly wind, a good surf piles into this sheltered beach, ripping worms and shellfish from the sands. Then is a good time to fish behind the surf from Newhaven's **East Pier**. Good cod are caught from here in winter, while the summer sees bass, mackerel, garfish, shad, mullet, and the usual smaller species. Most of these can be caught on the lightest of float tackle. To reach the pier, drive alongside the River Ouse towards the Sealink ferry terminal. Park near here and you'll see where the footpath crosses the railway line via a small concrete bridge.

This pier fishes best over the top of the tide. Bass, sea trout and the lesser predators come around in settled summer weather. Bass spread through the lower reaches of the estuary, particularly after dark, and when storms make the sea excessively rough. It is also likely that very big bass are hunting baitfish washed down by floodwater. The A259 road bridge and the turning berth upstream are both renowned marks.

Mullet can be found throughout this river. Access to the harbour is limited, although some of the best mullet fishing is in the main river, upstream at **Southease**. From here up to the freshwater, thin-lipped mullet may be found.

Lugworm may be dug from the sands inside Newhaven Arm. It offers similar fishing to that experienced from the East Pier, but is less popular with the small species. The problems here are: exposure to wind; the narrow, high wall; the band of concrete blocks that protect the wall from excessive pounding in rough seas; and the ropes of crab-pots set just beyond these blocks. It's often easier to fish at the very end, near the steps.

The slide-down rig baited with a small mackerel works well here. Float-fished prawns also appeal to the bass. Mackerel are abundant at times, throughout the tide. Herrings are feathered up here, usually late in the autumn if the weather stays settled. Conger may be caught here too,

Bass fishing is fair on the beach to the west of the Arm, particularly near the rocks at the far end. From here you can walk to **Old Nor**, a reef that sticks out into the tide and which attracts bass. Other reefs protrude from under the cliffs at **Peacehaven**, **Saltdean** and **Rottingdean**. Steps lead to the beach.

The rocks and sand patches off here are a major spawning ground for plaice in March. They don't feed then, but some big ones linger throughout the summer and provide pleasant surprises.

Brighton Marina now has easy access. Fishing is permitted on the seaward side of both piers, although the easterly arm is over a mile long, requiring an energetic walk. Cod, bass, conger, plaice, mackerel and a variety of other species are caught here, usually over the top of the tide. The outside of the longer arm offers excellent summer float fishing, particularly with small pouting and mackerel or live crabs and prawns for bass – and the occasional outsize pollack in the autumn.

Just past the marina, **Black Rock** marks the western end of the chalk reefs that begin at **Eastbourne**. As the A259 enters West Sussex, so the foreshore and the character of the fishing change. There are no significant reefs, just sand – mile upon mile of it all the way through to Hampshire. The fish-attracting features are therefore estuaries, tidal flows, channels, piers and other man-made structures.

Large black lugworm may be dug between the piers at Brighton, although no fishing is permitted on either of them – **The Palace Pier** has inadequate facilities, and the **West Pier** is derelict and dangerous. Dinghy fishermen are best placed to harvest the fish that visit these structures.

Close by the King Alfred swimming bath at **Hove** is a noted mark for January flounders. Small ragworm on light tackle score well. Many matches are fished over this stretch, but the easterly end produces best. Fair general fishing can be had along here, together with the odd bass when the water isn't pink with holidaymakers.

The harbour at **Southwick** isn't open for fishing, and the beaches in front are very bare and shallow. **Old Shoreham** power station has been shut down and is being demolished, so bass are no longer caught in the warm-water outfall. Dinghy anglers aren't happy to lose the station — the massive old chimneys were landmarks for fishermen from Newhaven through to Selsey.

Shoreham harbour offers better fishing. Bass run the river and are found around the sea defences at Southwick and the harbour mouth, particularly at low water. As the tide makes, they travel up the **River Adur**, and may be intercepted at bridges, wharves and where the main channel is accessible from the bank as far upriver as **Beeding**, where thin-lipped mullet may be caught.

The tidal flow in this estuary is the third fastest in Britain, so neap tides are preferred for fishing in the river. The flounder fishing can be excellent. Bass, soles, plaice, and the occasional conger and ray make up the better fishing here. Cod are very scarce in winter, although often abundant offshore, because the ground is too shallow to appeal to them. During the cold months the most frequent catches are whiting, pouting, flounders and dabs.

Small predators can be caught during the summer months from the harbour arms at Shoreham. Spinning, feathering, and float fishing with ultra-light tackle (by sea standards) are the preferred methods. Thick-lipped mullet are abundant around here.

The beaches at **Lancing**, **Worthing**, **Goring**, **Ferring** and **Rustington** are all exceptionally flat and sandy. However, find even the smallest point of interest and fish the surf there for bass. Plenty are caught along here, but they're generally small.

Otherwise the fishing is for flounders and dabs — and soles, after dark. However, two species are very fond of this part of the coast. Silver eels are abundant in spring. Match fishermen at **Goring** haul them in two at a time on peeler crab. These can be picked from ditches draining into the River Adur. Goring beach has a reputation for producing the better specimens of many different species.

In summer, the beaches from Lancing through to Ferring hold a strong attraction for migrating shoals of golden-grey mullet. These small fish, with the golden spot on the gill-covers, rarely grow over 2 lb, but sometimes turn the sea dark with their numbers. Naturally enough, trammel netsmen and beach seiners try to catch as many as possible. Nevertheless, those that survive offer good sport, particularly on ragworm baits around high water. The lighter the tackle, the greater the fun.

Worthing Pier offers fair fishing for bass, and a chance at mackerel and other small predators. Many plaice, flounders, dabs and other flatfish are caught here, together with eels. In winter, whiting and cod are taken, with less emphasis on the latter.

The sandflats warm up quickly when the sun shines in summer – the sort of conditions that rays like. Some dinghy anglers fish ridiculously light tackle for the thornbacks here. However, the one to tangle with for a tussle to remember is the stingray.

Some are caught each year on king ragworm from the beaches at **Littlehampton** and **Climping**. There's not much else on offer here other than little school bass, silver eels and dabs. At Littlehampton there's a large shingle bank which emerges on low spring tides. It's called **Winkle Island**. Ignore it because the tide moves fast and doesn't allow sufficient time for fishing. In fact, the airsea rescue helicopter knows its own way there now – many holidaymakers get cut off on this bank.

Littlehampton itself is famous for big bass, fishing from the gantry on the western side as the tide starts to push. Squid, mackerel and crab all produce fish. Further upriver, mullet are abundant – thick-lips in the saline zone, thins in the brackish water towards Arundel. Bass can be caught up there too, but watch the tide. It ebbs from this estuary at a ridiculous speed.

In many ways these Sussex estuaries are all the same – large bass come and go with the tide, and when they're not around, flounders, mullet, eels and schoolies fill the gap.

Middleton-on-Sea and **Bognor Regis** are famous for weed. It builds up after storms, and becomes very thick at times. However, it produces good fishing for those who know how to get the best results from the worst possible conditions.

The weed accumulates after storms on spring tides. Flies fill it with maggots, and when the next spring tides come along, the sea is filled with maggoty weed. To this feast come mullet, school bass and silver eels. The fishing isn't easy – but then is it ever? Results are what you make them.

Pagham harbour, available from the B2145 as it leads to Selsey, is a nature reserve. Thick-lipped mullet are abundant here, but are very hard to catch because of the lack of cover. Bass are available at the harbour mouth (there aren't any boats here nowadays) when the tide is low. Most of the standard techniques can be employed to lure them, but soft crab on an evening flood tide is probably the best way to score a satisfactory result. One of the better baits is slipper limpet, which you can gather from tidal pools on the shingly foreshore.

Selsey Bill offers reasonable mixed fishing. The water is deeper here, and this is reflected in the species that are available from this steep shingle beach. The tides are quicker, and reefs close to

A nicely marked ballan wrasse caught from the Kingmere Rocks off Littlehampton

shore attract bass, black bream, mackerel, and the usual run of summer species. Thornback rays are caught from the sandy parts.

At this point the A259 merges with the A27. The road to the Witterings is signposted, and takes you to the sands at **East** and **West Wittering** and **Bracklesham Bay**. It's all sand through here, and the spring tide strips it clean for hundreds of yards. And yet there are fish-attracting features – old peat beds, channels, and places where the tide obviously works a bit harder.

They all attract bass when a surf is running , although schoolies are usually found here. Sometimes a real chunk of a bass is caught, generally from July to October. Pack tope could be caught by anybody with enough line and patience. The best summer fish, though, is the sole. Plenty are caught here, but not by long casters. They travel the edge where the shingle meets the sand, where food accumulates in a fair tide and a sloppy sea, especially after a storm has provoked a bit of excitement. Flounders, dabs, small black bream and eels are also available.

The tide race at the mouth of **Wittering harbour** is noted for bass and the occasional smoothhound. Slipper limpet in the surf is the classic bait here, although crab and other highly-scented attractors guide the fish through the enormous acreage of sand and dirty water. Slippers are abundant here – you can find masses along the sands after a storm, and drifts of them at the mouth of Wittering Harbour.

Chichester harbour, around to **Thorney Island**, offers flounders, eels and the hope that an enormous bass will engulf the bait. Some very big specimens are caught each year from these tranquil, unspoilt bays. Unfortunately this sea area isn't too large when the mudflats strip at low tide, and the better specimens of other species are more frequently encountered out to sea.

This doesn't prevent the bass from harvesting all the crabs, eels, mullets, flounders, sandeels and other goodies that are too succulent to defend themselves. These big fish take up residence, living here all summer alongside bass fry that were born 25 generations later.

These residents leave only when the chill of winter flushes them out. They're few, and a tough proposition. So good luck!

Boat tackle and techniques

BOAT fishing can be divided into two categories – inshore and deep-sea. Many of the inshore techniques are the same as those used off the beach, except with less emphasis on casting.

Deep-sea boat fishing requires an extension to the armoury. A range of conventional boat rods may be called into service, but most anglers use something around 20–30 lb class for bottom fishing for cod, tope and rays. When trolling for bass or fishing for plaice and soles, a lighter rod is preferable.

A 50 lb class rod is the choice of many wreck anglers. It has sufficient backbone to work large pirks and to handle heavy weights when fishing with bait. A fairly meaty rod is required to haul big cod, ling and conger away from the structure before they tangle with an old net or length of rusting hawser.

For this type of fishing, a powerful reel is needed – one that can handle the fish and the depth of water. Load it with 40 lb line – that will prove easier to break when the tackle does snag the wreck. Line for wrecking should be hard, to reduce abrasion, and low-stretch, for maximum control over tackle and fish.

The lighter boat rods work well with small to medium beach reels loaded with the appropriate line. Even so, it is possible to be completely ridiculous at times and fish with light freshwater leger tackle for small fish like black bream, dabs and whiting. When the bigger lumps are refusing to put in an appearance, the gap is best filled by catching tiddlers on flimsy tackle.

The uptide casting outfit is becoming more popular each year, but isn't widely used off Sussex because deep water is so readily available to boat anglers. Nevertheless, there is plenty of shallow ground where uptide fishing techniques produce better results than conventional down tide fishing.

When trying for large fish like tope and conger on conventional down tide tackle, it frequently pays to cast a smaller bait uptide for small fish like plaice, black bream, dogfish and so on. This is particularly meaningful when tope fishing. These are generally released at the boatside, so the uptide rod permits a few fish to be caught for the table: the irony of tope fishing is that, even when sport is brilliant, one goes home fishless.

The tides around this coast aren't too severe, so there is no need to spool up with wire line. However, it permits less lead to be used when fishing bait beside a deep-water wreck. Many charter skippers dislike braided polyester line, particularly for wrecking, because it chafes, snaps, and tangles other lines so readily.

Fortunately there is never much difficulty in getting mackerel for bait during the summer months. These arrive in May and throng close to shore during June and July, depending on the weather. Unsettled conditions drive them offshore, but they're generally somewhere out there through to November, especially in an Indian summer.

A box of mackerel can be processed in several ways. Whole fillets are used for tope and turbot, half fillets for bass and dogfish, narrow, silvery strips for bream and other small fish. Small whole fish make ideal tope baits, especially if stabbed repeatedly with a knife to release the juices.

The standard bait for wrecking is a mackerel 'flapper'. This is a whole fish, filleted towards the head from the tail, breaking off the spine behind the gills. The two fillets are firmly attached, but are free to flap in the tide.

Mackerel also make good groundbait for some forms of fishing. Cut the fish into slices, like a cucumber. A very sharp knife with a serrated edge makes light work of this and prevents an aching wrist.

The guts of a cuttle fish are preferred by one of Newhaven's top skippers when fishing for conger and big cod. This bait has boated him several cod over 40 lb. The rest of the cuttlefish works, too, as does squid. Pouting is an effective bait for conger. Inshore, soft crab is very good, particularly the edible and velvet swimming crabs that are abundant under the chalk cliffs.

Wreck fishing with pirks and feathers produces huge bags of cod and ling. Silver, black, and yellow pirks, weighing 1–2 lb, work well below a string of four feathers tied on 8/0 hooks and 80 lb line. The fish may be lying immediately uptide of the wreck, along its side, or some distance astern. The boat's electronics and the skipper's experience help to locate them and keep tackle away from snags. Pirks should be worked very close to the bottom. Sometimes cod strike best when the pirk isn't jigged at all.

Wreck fishing at anchor requires heavy leads to ensure positive contact with terminal tackle and to prevent tangles.

Weights should be conical in shape, not like flattened diamonds, which catch the tide. Traces are generally six feet of 300 lb nylon line, with an 8/0 Model Perfect hook crimped one end, a swivel at the other. Wire traces are seldom used, except for tope and sharks.

The weight is on a sliding boom, and may be fixed to this with weaker nylon in case of tangles. Sensitivity is essential. At these depths, a gentle knock may be from a very large fish. Let it have line and time to engulf the bait before setting the hook.

Similar tackle, but on a lighter scale, is adequate for most inshore fishing at anchor. When tope fishing, an 18-inch trace of 200 lb wire solves the tooth problem. Attach this to eight feet of 80 lb line to take the chafing from its skin. Many tope anglers fix a sliding boom on the main line for the weight, but stop it 20 feet from the trace with a bead and a stop made from 25 close-touching turns of fine telephone wire. Thus a very long trace wafts appealingly in the tide. The stop can be slackened off, allowing the sinker to slide down to the trace when bringing fish alongside.

Boat casting in these waters rarely requires more than a 6 oz lead to grip bottom. In some places, where the water is deep, it is necessary to cast further uptide than usual, lest the tackle be washed astern before it reaches the bottom. When using this technique, make sure you fish from the up-wind side. With the breeze pushing the boat at an angle across the tide, baits on the up-wind side are carried away from the boat by the current, while baits cast uptide from the down-wind side are carried back under the boat.

Trolling and drifting with Red Gills, plug fishing, spinning, bait fishing with dabs, pouting, squid, mackerel and crab, and float trolling with joey mackerel, all produce outsize bass each year. These specialised techniques are generally practised by dedicated anglers from their own boats.

Best of the boat marks

BOAT fishing is very popular off the Sussex coast for two reasons. Firstly, there's a sophisticated fleet of charter boats, and clubs

Boat anglers hunt for bass under the white cliffs of Beachy Head

from as far as London, Hertfordshire and Middlesex have regular bookings. These craft operate out of **Rye, Newhaven, Brighton** marina, **Shoreham**, and **Littlehampton**.

The second reason is that the shingle beaches along this coastline are ideal for small boats. Some belong to local angling clubs, while others can be hired by the day. Launching is restricted by the tides, but dozens of fishing hulls are to be seen at **Hastings, St Leonards, Bexhill, Pevensey Bay, Langney Point**, near Eastbourne, **Seaford, Brighton, Hove, Shoreham, Worthing, Bognor Regis** and **Selsey**. The harbours at Rye, Newhaven, Brighton, Shoreham, Littlehampton and Chichester also have extensive flotillas of boats.

Launching facilities for 'trailer-sailors' in this county are both scarce and inadequate; consequently, most anglers have to rely on the services of a charter skipper. There are plenty to choose from, at different rates of hire, and various degrees of competence. We'll look at what's on offer at the different centres.

Boats leaving **Rye harbour**, to the south of the town, have a wide choice of fishing. Numerous sand and shingle banks offer tope, spurdogs, rays, turbot and similar fish during the summer months. Sometimes shoals of cod appear on banks like the **Bullock Bank** and can be caught on lightweight pirks.

However, the best offshore fishing in these parts is over the numerous wrecks littered around out there. They offer good fishing for cod, conger, and ling on pirks and bait.

During the winter months, anglers fish worm and shellfish around the banks and more open ground close to land, and haul up large numbers of cod. The sandy beaches on each side of the harbour are riddled with big black lugworm, while razorfish, queen cockles, mussels and whelks are washed up after storms. They make useful cocktail baits.

One of the favourite winter fishing grounds is the **West Road**, the strip of sea that stretches from Rye bay eastwards to **Dungeness Point**. This area is also excellent for sole fishing in summer, confirmed by the masses of trammel nets to be seen here.

In summer, the general ground fishing is for tope, rays, turbot, plaice, soles, small conger, black bream and dogfish, and the usual run of lesser species. The offshore seabed between **Rye** and **Eastbourne** is shallow and undulating. There are banks of sand and shingle, like the **Four Fathom Ridge** off Hastings. These, and the channels between them, offer reasonable fishing throughout the year. From October through to February, the cod fishing is good, depending on the strength of the season. Plenty of big fish are caught from holes amid the reefs.

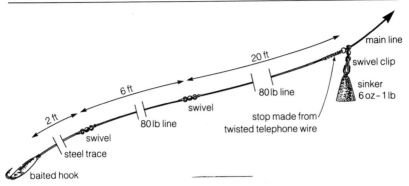

Figure 6 Tope tackle for boat fishing

Off **Fairlight**, west of Hastings, areas of reef and boulder banks offer good mixed summer fishing. These patches extend westwards towards **Beachy Head**, near Eastbourne, where numerous reefs offer bass, pollack, and conger fishing. The **Horse of Willingdon**, the **Copper Shoals** and the **Royal Sovereign** shoals are the best known. Small inshore wrecks, like the **Barnhill** off Langney Point, are noted for producing large bass on legered fish baits.

Beachy Head offers excellent bass fishing on baits and artificial lures over the Ledge, which extends two miles under the sea from this famous landmark. Turbulent tides along this coast produce heavy overfalls around the Head. Shoals of baitfish – mackerel, scad, sprats, herring, and sandeels – send bass and cod into feeding frenzies on occasion. Tope frequent the gullies further offshore. However, fishing is usually poor at the peak of spring tides because the currents are so strong.

The high standard of the wreck fishing attracts most interest along this stretch of coast. There are dozens of wrecks in this sea area, and uncharted ones are discovered every year. Even so, Rye is not the most important harbour for charter boats along this coast. Its drawback is that the harbour bar is too shallow at low tide for most boats to negotiate.

Anglers who fish out from **Hastings** or **Eastbourne** may join two large sea angling clubs. Both have substantial clubhouses on the beach and offer self-drive dinghy hire to those who don't have their own boat parked in the club's compound.

A new marina is currently being built at **Langney Point**, to the east of Eastbourne, which will make these prolific grounds considerably more accessible to fishermen of all persuasions. This is bound to increase the pressures on stocks.

Boats fishing out of **Newhaven** produce phenomenal catches from time to time. Some of the skippers are livewires and consistently find large numbers of fish for their anglers. Others are close to retirement and couldn't care tuppence whether their anglers catch much at all.

As usual, the considerate skippers are heavily booked by regular parties. These 'frequent fliers' are the mainstay of a skipper's business and are well catered for. Anglers wishing for the best results are advised to club together and take regular bookings throughout the year.

Obviously it is unrealistic to expect to go out with a top skipper on the best tides of the year unless you support him when the fish are less thick on the ground. After all, skippers have families to feed. They're unimpressed by people who only phone when the fishing is brilliant and the boat could be filled several times over.

Boats from Newhaven take anglers trolling for bass and bait fishing for tope off Beachy Head. In summer, many boats go far out over the **Ledge**, to where the seabed falls away dramatically about a dozen miles offshore. Here they take large cod in winter, spurdogs and other dogfish, some rays, the occasional turbot and brill, small congers, and the usual run of small fish. These include whiting, pouting, black bream, plaice, dabs, gurnard and the like.

Wreck fishing produces good cod all year round, although unsettled conditions generally prohibit long trips offshore during the colder months. In summer − and if there is no EEC ban on cod fishing − huge hauls are frequently made. Skippers use spells of fine weather to make extended trips to remote wrecks − by day and night. Believe it or not, brilliant cod fishing with pirks is to be had after dark!

Few of these wrecks offer significant pollack fishing, although plenty are caught. They're not as big as those found at the western end of the Channel, although double-figure specimens do turn up. Doubtless, more would be caught if they were fished for deliberately.

However, most anglers are after cod and big bottom feeders, so don't give themselves much chance to catch pollack. Around dusk, clouds of them feed above some of the distant wrecks. Sometimes the fish are so dense that the echo-sounder can barely distinguish the hulk beneath. At such times a Red Gill on a long trace produces excellent sport.

The ling off Sussex are quite small from inshore wrecks − rarely much more than low double-figures. However, the bigger deep-water wrecks produce hefty chunks weighing 20−30 lb. They're caught on big baits and baited pirks fished tight to the wreck − and the seabed.

A big bass comes aboard amid a flurry of spray

These tactics also produce congers – and large ones. Plenty of 60–80 lb fish are landed each year, and almost as many escape back down to the seabed because the angler has panicked. These large and powerful fish are not easy to bring to boat, and many a 'telegraph pole' has smashed the tackle and ripped itself off the gaff at boatside. Big fish like this must be played out completely in midwater.

Much the same sort of ground is to be found off **Brighton** – open ground interspersed with patches of reef, banks and deeper holes, with the offshore wrecks offering anglers their best chance of catching something very big.

The Pipe, a mile off Saltdean, is an area of rocky ground that offers sheltered winter cod fishing during a stiff nor'easter, and good summer bass and conger fishing. **The Mill** mark, four miles off the windmill on the cliff behind the marina, is a bank where the depth rises from 45 feet to 20 feet. It produces good bags of spurdogs, some bream, and reasonable general fishing.

Rock Toe, a mile and a quarter off the Palace Pier, produces big bass, conger, wrasse and small pollack. Farther west is **Looe Gate**, a mile and three-quarters offshore. It's a big reef that's noted for conger and black bream – and occasionally produces outsize stingrays.

There's not much wreck fishing out from **Shoreham** because the boats have to travel too far to reach the productive deep-water structures. Indeed, from here through the **Selsey**, the really deep water lies farther and farther offshore. This is the land of sand-flats – a largely sterile plain that is broken by occasional banks, wrecks, gullies and similar fish-attracting features.

These sandflats produce large stingrays from time to time, along with thornbacks and occasional small-eyed rays. Tope, small conger, turbot and the lesser species may readily be taken on tackle as light as 12 lb class. Even on a big spring tide, no more than 8 oz weights are required.

One of the best-known marks off this part of Sussex is the **Kingmere Rocks**, an extensive area of heavy reef with a few small wrecks on it, lying in fairly shallow water about four miles off **Littlehampton**.

It is noted for its black bream, although these have been hammered since the cod ban forced commercial fishermen to pursue other species. Rock-hopper trawls make large catches of these poor-tasting, hard-fighting fish. The reef's congers, however, respond well to night fishing, especially if a trail of groundbait is put down to encourage them.

At **Selsey Bill**, boats have a useful tide-race in which to fish

The rewards of wrecking. A party of London anglers with a massive catch of cod taken aboard the *Nikaria* out of Newhaven. Dave Jarvis (*centre*) holds the best at 46 lb 2 oz!

Big cod do take livebaits. This 22-pounder had a taste for pouting

natural and artificial baits for bass, both in midsummer and in the autumn. Fast tides running through the deeper offshore channels, like those off Beachy Head, prove very attractive to tope during the early part of summer.

Chichester harbour is a handy place for dinghy fishing. During midsummer heatwaves, mackerel sometimes blitz the fry as far up as **Bosham** (pronounced 'Bozum'). Under these conditions, big bass are known to follow them.

The harbour offers plenty of fishing for eels, small black bream, and thick-lipped mullet and smoothhounds are occasionally caught in the deep channels at **Itchenor** and **West Wittering**. Bass can be caught in the many bays and plenty of schoolies use this harbour. However, the problem when fishing big baits for lunkers is that millions of crabs live here, too.

Some of the best dinghy fishing is in winter, though, when the flounders are fattening up ready to spawn. Baited spoons sort out the larger specimens, fished on sporty tackle behind a drifting boat. The bait should be a wriggling bunch of harbour ragworms. These can readily be dug – where permitted – from the foreshore mudflats.

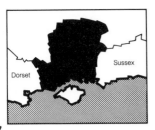

Richard Stapley

HAMPSHIRE

FAREHAM'S Richard Stapley is our guide to the Hampshire coast. A very keen boat angler, he also likes to get to grips with the shore cod come winter time. He is a regular contributor to *Sea Angler* magazine.

A COAST THAT OFFERS EVERYTHING

THE Hampshire coastline is not spectacular; there is nothing to compare with the majestic cliffs of Beachy Head or the rugged grandeur of Portland Bill. However, there is a good variety of sport available to shore anglers, and an even better range of options afloat.

For the beach angler, flounders are found in quality and quantity to compare with anywhere, there is excellent sole fishing, and reasonable numbers of plaice and dabs. Smoothhound and stingray can be taken from certain beaches, there are bass, small-eyed rays, black bream, cod, whiting, pout, silver eels, mackerel, garfish and all the grey mullets, including the rare golden-grey: other species are encountered from time to time, but these are the main targets.

Offshore, tope sport is outstanding in season, and although the bass has been hard hit by netting and commercial 'angling', excellent results can be enjoyed still by drift lining live sandeels to the shoaling fish. Conger, spurdog, all the rays, brill and turbot, porbeagle and thresher sharks, and, from the offshore wrecks, pollack and ling can be added to the above catalogue, along with endless dogfish.

The Hampshire coastline can conveniently be divided into open sea beaches, comprising the stretch from Hayling Island to Portsmouth harbour mouth, then from Hurst Castle to the county boundary at Chewton Bunny; solent beaches, covering Portsmouth harbour mouth to Hurst; and the creeks and harbours of Chichester, Langstone, Portsmouth, Southampton Water and Lymington. These different environments have their own ebb and flow of seasonal species.

The angling year begins in spring – March in most years. Plaice, returning from spawning, gather off Hayling and Eastney in particular, before percolating into the Solent and the lower reaches of the harbours during April and May. Close to the beach, they will be joined by returning flounders, whilst offshore their main companions will be the dab. April sees bass, mullet and silver eels coming within reach of the shore angler, whilst the harbours quickly refill with flounders as well as these three species.

Although flounders are taken bottom fishing in early season, throughout the summer the most effective technique – often by a ratio of 20 fish to one – is the baited spoon, a method developed in the muddy waters of Fareham Creek and now established as *the* method for the species at this time.

May brings the season alive with a bang. Boat anglers see the arrival of tope, smoothhound, turbot, rays, spurdog and bass, all following the migrating sandeel and mackerel shoals, and also the black bream, which comes to spawn on the shallow chalk reefs. Shore anglers expect small-eyed ray from May onwards, with smoothhound and stingray featuring during June. Soles begin to appear on open beaches and from the Solent, and the wrecks harbour pollack, with cod also present for a few weeks.

July sees black bream patrolling certain beaches, sometimes small ones only, sometimes decent fish of 1 lb or more. Conger are increasingly active on offshore reefs and wrecks, whilst ling are also present in growing numbers. The dog days of August and September can be a bit dull. Push 25 miles or more out and the wrecks can be good, while the beach man can sneak out soles at night, mackerel, gars or bass at first light or dusk, but overall high-water temperatures and lots of weed and crabs do nothing for angling results.

The first frosts of October see a fresh improvement. Autumnal gales bring cod and whiting inshore to forage. In boom codling years, Hampshire gets its share from beach and boat, but the county's special pride are the very big winter fish taken from Needles and Nab marks. Each year sees specimens over 35 lb, with one or two likely to top the magic 40 lb. In a typical season, the average fish weighs 16–25 lb, but they are not plentiful, and four cod on the boat is a good result. Sport usually peaks around Christmas and declines fairly sharply in the New Year as mature fish depart to spawn, although the best chance of a truly gigantic cod lies in finding a late spawner about now.

With the departure of bass, mullet and eels from the harbours in November, the flounder settles again to a bottom-feeding role as it packs on weight and condition prior to moving offshore to spawn late in January or early February. For a month, the beaches belong to immature flounders, dabs, whiting, pout or rockling, and then the year has come full circle.

A word about tides may not be out of place. The combination of the Isle of Wight disrupting tidal flow and the numerous harbours filling and emptying means that tides are frequently very strong and always complex, particularly around the Solent.

A case in point is the 'west run', a phenomenon associated with the best inshore fishing in the East Solent. As the main push of flood tide runs west to east along the English Channel, it is divided by the Wight, some entering the Solent via the Hurst Race and much more roaring round the back of the Wight and then sweeping into the Solent from the east. A dinghy angler off Eastney will find the west run starting two hours before high water at Portsmouth and ending five hours later, on spring tides. The last of the west run reaches Southamptom after the ebb has begun and produces the famous second high water.

The combination of hard tides and shallow water means that a change of tidal direction can result in a force 4 breeze that had previously raised hardly a ripple suddenly putting up a really nasty short, steep sea. The transformation can happen in minutes and the dinghy angler needs always to be aware of this. Ebbing spring tides in Portsmouth, Chichester and Langstone harbours are torrential and an under-engined boat will not make headway. Wind against tide is bad news for small vessels and care must be taken.

Tackle and techniques for shore fishing

MANY Hampshire anglers fish quite contentedly with a single powerful beach outfit. It is effective enough for most species, but greater enjoyment and variety can be had from fishing with a wider range of tackle.

Nevertheless, the basic starting point must be a conventional surf rod balanced to 5−6 oz leads. There is not the same emphasis on sheer distance as the key to success as in some other areas of the country − true, cod and small-eyed rays often demand the ability to present a big bait in the 100−130-yard band, but many other fish habitually swim very much closer to the shingle. Any of the modern 12−13-foot rods geared to the pendulum or extended off-ground cast will be more than adequate for the task. Daiwa produce a fine range of rods, though many anglers prefer to build their own around one of the blanks available from firms like Zziplex, Conoflex, Century or North Western. Virtually all tackle shops can have rods made up to your specifications, if you prefer.

There is no rough ground worthy of the name off any Hampshire beach; the worst seabed you are likely to cast into is broken flints or mussel beds, and clean sand, shingle or mud is more usual. Thus there is no need for heavy-duty reels, and the choice falls between small to medium multipliers or saltwater-sized fixed spools − personal preference should be the deciding factor. Most anglers who choose the multiplier have opted for the ABU 6000 or 7000 series reels or the Daiwa 6HM, all with the level-wind removed. The new generation of beach reels like the Shimano Speedmaster and the Daiwa SL20H have rapidly established a toehold and may well prove to be the reels of the 1990s. Mainlines of 12−18 lb breaking strain are perfectly adequate for fish and terrain, coupled, of course, with a shock leader of 50−60 lb.

Although the above tackle will cope with any Hampshire beach situation, a lighter bottom outfit will provide better sport in the harbours and on many of the Solent beaches. A rod to cast 2−4 oz is the tool for the task unless you are fishing into an onshore gale or near gale, when the smaller lead lacks the momentum to carry the bait out far enough. Once there were a wide variety of suitable rods on the market, but with the general decline of surf bass fishing the options are rather limited, although suitable 'bass' rods are available from Daiwa and Zziplex. Fixed-spool reels do not sit well on these light rods and a small multiplier is preferred, teamed with 10−12 lb line and a 25−40 lb leader, depending on the lead being cast.

Finally, there is some very enjoyable fishing to be had in summer and early autumn, float fishing from suitable vantage points or spinning a wobbling spoon, plug or plastic sandeel for mackerel, garfish, scad or bass. The best weapons for the task come from freshwater fishing; carp or pike rods, or a salmon spinning rod around 10 feet long. A small to medium fixed-spool reel loaded with 6−9 lb line allows the angler to belt lures in the ½−1 oz range a country mile, or to persuade a big balsa-wood floating plug to travel the surprisingly short distance needed to get into bass country. It will handle float tackle pretty well, too, although a longer rod of 12 feet allows better line pick-up and control and may be a worthwhile investment if you plan to fish farther west than Hampshire, where the float is essentially a minor tactic.

The same rod can be pressed into service for mullet fishing, unless you are one of that breed of mullet fanatics who devote their every waking hour to plotting the downfall of this most challenging quarry. If you are, you'll want a float rod, a leger rod and, more than likely, a toothpick spinning rod as well for fishing a baited bar-spoon. This takes us into the realms of specialisation and rather beyond the scope of this book.

Even the more enlightened Hampshire beach anglers probably spend 95 per cent of their time bottom fishing; for consistent results it has proven to be the right approach. Two very straightforward rigs cover my requirements for most of this fishing. For distance casting for cod or rays, or for general big fish work in search of smoothhounds, stingers or bass, I use a single-hook paternoster with the bait clipped down in the slipstream of the lead. Even when great distance is not required this minimises bait damage. A hook length of 24–30 inches allows a big fish to suck in the bait to the back of the mouth before being brought up short by the resistance of the lead wires and thus hooking itself. On certain Solent beaches, wired leads are often unnecessary, and here the longer snood permits a little more bait movement in the shallow and relatively tide-free water.

Small fish work, for whiting, pout, flatfish, bream and the like, is tackled with a two- or three-hook paternoster. I use the very neat Avis booms or the similar gadgets from Pro-Rig to provide the stand-off pieces. Hook snoods of six to eight inches are about right, and 20–30 lb nylon keeps tangles to a minimum and reduces twisting by 'spinning' pout or silver eels. Harbour fishing can sometimes demand a 'one up one down' rig with a hook fishing in the wake of the lead. Using a plain lead, allowing it either to roll around in the tide or inch-retrieving it, flounders approaching to investigate the stirred-up mud are more than likely to encounter one or other bait. When the water is clear, it may pay to reduce the snood strength to 12–15 lb, especially in frosty conditions.

One other instance when a long, light trace may score is for spring plaice fishing. Very low water temperatures at the start of the season sometimes mean that the plaice will only take a small bait on a size 3 or 4 hook on a trace of only 6–8 lb. Hooks for the heavier fishing are Mustad 79515 or Cox + Rawle Uptides between 2/0 and 5/0, while for the lighter work an Aberdeen type between 4 and 1/0 is about right. My current favourite is the eyed version of the famous Mustad Aberdeen Blue, model 37275.

Settled anticyclonic weather in summer and early autumn – well, we must get some one year – can reduce beach fishing prospects to depressingly poor levels. However, float fishing around the piers or harbour mouths at dawn or dusk can provide enjoyable sport with mackerel and garfish, sometimes small pollack or even a bass. A straightforward sliding float rig, set at around three feet for garfish, six to 12 feet for mackerel, is all that is needed.

Hampshire is very fortunate in that virtually all major baits are available from its shores. Undoubtedly the most used bait is the king ragworm, which is present in good numbers in all the harbours and much of the Solent, especially in the Lepe area west of Southamptom. For years there has been a thriving industry exporting these worms around the country, and every local tackle

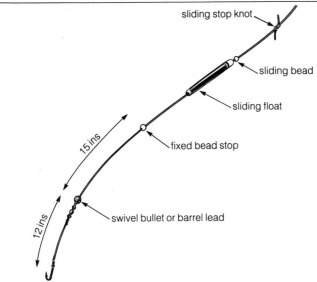

Figure 7 Sliding float rig

shop stocks them, although you will almost certainly need to order in advance at weekends. Constant digging pressure means that the worms seldom achieve colossal size, usually peaking at 8–10 inches, but this scarcely worries the shore angler, who often finds three or four small worms a more effective bait.

King ragworm is a successful bait for all the small species and most of the large, particularly the stingray. Even cod, not noted for their love of ragworm, take it with some freedom. Only confirmed fish eaters like small-eyed rays and turbot are likely to pass it by, and even they will succumb from time to time. Tiny harbour rag (also known as mud rag, creeper or jumper rag) are well distributed in muddy areas just below the high water mark and, particularly, in the tidal reaches of freshwater streams. Delicate and unsuited to distance casting, it is a fine bait for flounder, bass and soles.

Silver rag are present in small numbers in all the lug beds, but as ever with this bait the major concentrations are very localised. The man prepared to search could do worse than start looking at Lee-on-Solent and Hill Head. It is a good bait which can at times provide an important edge in competition fishing, and plaice in particular relish it. However, for pleasure fishing, possession of 'snakes' is seldom a prerequisite of success.

There are far fewer lug beds in Hampshire than there are ragworm colonies, and worms are only small to medium blow lug.

Very heavy digging pressure following the codling boom years of 1986–8 has severely damaged the beds and it is hard to assess how long recovery will take. Lugworm is a good bait for sole and plaice, and dabs like it, but the local flounders show precious little enthusiasm. It comes into its own as an autumn and winter bait for whiting and cod, when many local shops import black lug, yellowtails, and big blow lug for sale. It comes from Kent, Wales and even Belgium!

Peeler crab is plentiful enough in the harbours, green shore crabs being the species. With a shortage of obvious rocky areas most of them bury themselves in the mud and regular crabbers provide cover in the form of pieces of guttering or roof tiles. The peeler crabs ideal home makes an ideal trap, but you'll need to find an out of the way place to set them. Hermit crabs are also a good bait, and can be drop-netted from piers in modest quantities. Some commercial whelk potters and trawlermen get plenty, and you might be able to strike up an agreement for a pint or two. Crab is far and away the best bait for smoothhounds, and is also good for cod, bass, stingray and silver eels.

Shellfish has its moments, mainly on open sea beaches during or just after a heavy onshore blow. Slipper limpet is the traditional and successful bait, and can be picked up in vast quantities from Hayling and Hill Head. Clams have come into prominence in recent seasons, with cod in particular finding them hard to resist.

Sandeels are seine netted from Langstone and Chichester harbours, and most shops stock the flash-frozen products from Ammo or Starmer Bait Supplies. Live eels, fresh-killed or frozen, usually in that order, are the bait for small-eyed rays and small turbot, and will also take bass and whiting amongst others. Small eels, float-fished, are good for mackerel and garfish.

Fish or squid strips in various sizes will account for most species, including dabs, whiting, pout, mackerel and black bream. Pout are themselves a major food item for the small-eyed ray, and a fillet, or head and guts, is a popular local bait. For the serious-minded big bass hunter, a live pout, huge fillet of fresh mackerel, or a whole squid gives the opportunity of a big fish at the price of the inevitable blank sessions.

Guide to shore venues – the open sea and Solent beaches

HAYLING **Island** has a beach frontage of some three miles, bounded by the sandbanks at Eastoke Point, to the east, and the East

The flatfish fishing in the Solent can be lively. Chris Clark swings in two
flounders from the Netley reaches. Southampton docks can just be seen in
the background

Winner Bank, to the west. It is a shingle beach giving quickly on to sand, and carries a heavy surf when the wind blows south-west round to south-east.

There is deep water between Black Point and Eastoke Point, where the main channel of Chichester harbour empties into the open sea. Countless sailing dinghies and board sailors make the area a madhouse on summer weekends, but dawn and dusk in the July-September period can see the water come alive, especially at high tide. Millions of bait fish are often herded by launce and mackerel, and big bass are prepared to hit anything smaller than themselves. Spinning with plug, wobbling spoon or plastic sandeel can give super sport.

For a mile or so at **Eastoke**, the shingle has been artificially built up as a sea defence. It is rapidly being eroded again, but is presently much steeper than the rest of the beach. When there are plenty of codling around (and that depends on breeding success producing a strong year class) there is very good autumn and winter sport to be had, particularly when there is a big surf running. Standard codding tactics, long casting at night with lugworm bait, prove the most effective although ragworm and shellfish also score. In calm conditions, fishing at 50−75 yards with scaled-down hooks and baits finds whiting, pout and flatfish. Summer fishing is indifferent, mainly silver eels, pout and flatties at night, with occasional bass, bream or smoothhound.

The stretch from Eastoke corner along to the funfair at **Beachlands** is much less steep, but still produces cod in good seasons. It is especially good for bass in autumn storms, fishing bunched slipper limpet at ridiculously close ranges. From Beachlands to the **Chichester Avenue** car park can produce super night fishing in January and February, with plentiful flounders, some dabs, plaice, pout and whiting. Four-hour matches sometimes need 30 flounders to win.

Best results for flounders here come on spring tides, fishing four hours to high water and two back. The codding to the east runs from an hour or so before high down the ebb, and perhaps for the young flood as well. Bass tend to take best at low tide and on the first of the flood.

Farther to the west a degree of shelter from a sou'wester comes from the Isle of Wight and from the East Winner, which absorbs some of the fury of the waves. It is worth a try when conditions are really bad, although it is a bit of a weed trap. The **East Winner** itself is extremely shallow and usually carries some surf − bass range over it on a flooding tide and can be taken on sandeel bait.

Flounder fishing is fun. England man Chris Clark with two fine samples taken on a moving worm bait

Langstone harbour entrance is fouled by a disgusting sewage outfall which discharges on the ebb tide. Nevertheless, a wide variety of species do work the deep channel scoured out by the tide, and if the floating weed is not too bad sport can be quite reasonable. The tide is *very* strong and best results come either side of a low- and high-water slack.

Moving across to the Portsmouth side, we find the **West Winner Bank**, a much smaller and narrower bank made up of big pebbles. Fishing the beach east of this bank for some 200–300 yards can produce very good flounder sport from mid-March to early May. Fish a spring tide, four hours up and two back with ragworm bait. Don't be depressed by slow results, the fish here can switch on or off in dramatic fashion, and you may take half a dozen on successive casts between long blank spells.

There are far fewer flounders west of the Bank, but some plaice are to be had during spring. The best plaice fishing is generally on the stretch of beach in front of the pitch and putt golf course at St George's Road. There is a mussel bed out there, which produces plaice to 3 lb or so, sometimes larger, from March to May. Fish daylight tides, ideally on a calm sunny day, two hours up and four back. The plaice will feed at any time, but will often go best as the strong west run eases in the last couple of hours. King or silver rag are good baits.

The beach gets very crowded in summer, but night fishing will give pout, lots of silver eels, occasional bass and flatfish. Autumn and winter night tides are good for whiting, and in the better years, codling.

Fishing is permitted from **South Parade Pier** on payment of a modest fee, daylight through to mid-evening only. The pier offers a few plaice in spring, with the best recorded over 5 lb. Some cod are to be had in winter, but overall the pier is not a good area. A few mackerel, garfish and plenty of small pollack can be caught in summer and early autumn.

West of the pier, **Southsea Beach** itself is highly popular with holidaymakers in summer. There is fair spring fishing for plaice and flounders on daylight tides, especially at the storm drain, in the middle of the beach, and at the far end adjoining Southsea Castle. Fish the spring tides two or three hours each side of high water.

The steep and often slippery sea defences around Southsea Castle can be dangerous, for the water is deep and the tide strong. Round the corner, by the Model Railway, you can fish summer evening tides from low water up for pout, silver eels and a few big soles, mainly at short range.

Clarence Beach, in front of the Cenotaph, is one of the few out and out low-water marks in Hampshire. Fish two hours either side of low in September or October, night tides, of course. There are soles at 60 yards or so, along with plaice, dabs, pout and eels. If it's a bit lumpy, a bait fished at 20–30 yards may well find a bass or two.

Clarence Pier itself has a funfair, and to me encapsulates all that is worst about the British seaside holiday. Fishing is banned, not that I would want to do so in summer. Once the pier closes in October, there is no one to prevent you sampling the autumn and winter sport. The shipping channel comes within casting range, and you can catch pout, cod and occasionally conger to 15 lb or so.

West of the pier lies an old moat, part of the City's ancient defences, and beyond that the **Square Tower** is a vantage point that can fish for flounders and plaice in spring. As the weed problem grows in summer, so the very hard tide makes fishing increasingly difficult.

The tiny **Victoria Pier** is usually crowded with anglers of varying competence catching little, but in late summer and early autumn a tide that starts to ebb around first light will sometimes give an hour or two of hectic sport with small pollack, mackerel, garfish and sometimes a bass. Mullet also haunt the pier and can be caught on float-fished bread over a bag of bread groundbait.

The harbour mouth itself has very heavy traffic: cross-Channel ferries, container ships, the Royal Navy and endless yachts. Fishing at the **Round Tower**, **Pickfords Beach** or across the water at **HMS Dolphin** can produce bass of all sizes, including very big. The normal tactic is to fish a livebait at close range, but spinning a plug, sandeel or wobbling spoon can also pay off.

Access to all Portsmouth and Hayling beaches is very easy; there are good seafront roads and as long as you don't go during the day between May and September, parking is easy.

The steep sea wall at **Haslar** is not without its dangers — it can be slippery in the rain or frost and it has a few broken bones to its credit. Mullet work Haslar around high water in summer and can be caught on bread. Most locals opt for the autumn and winter sport, which gives a good variety of species, but particularly whiting, pout and cod — the latter can be big fish well into double figures. An ebbing tide at night is preferred, with lug, crab or squid.

Another good spot for cod are the groynes immediately west of Fort Monckton, although weed is often a problem. Other species include dabs, pout, whiting and bass. Spring plaice fishing can be good, and a few years back I had eight totalling 25 lb down the ebb after three hours without a bite.

Gilkicker Point produces similar fishing, and once around the corner **Stokes Bay** down as far as the 'built-up' section of sea wall offers deep water and relatively little tide. When conditions are bad and most beaches weeded up, Stokes is my banker for a fishable spot. It's not that great, the usual modest pout, whiting, flats and silver eels, with occasional cod and bass. Best fishing October–December, on the last four hours of a flooding spring tide.

After a short shallow section at the west end of Stokes Bay, the water drops away again off **Browndown Ranges** – don't enter when the red flags are flying. This is a useful spot for plaice, cod, whiting and the usual species, best in autumn and winter.

The sleepy seaside town of **Lee-on-Solent** yields a few flounders and odd big plaice in spring. Late summer and early autumn sees a fair number of soles, with the area adjoining the hovercraft slipway at *HMS Daedalus* popular. A good onshore blow in autumn can give respectable bags of school bass to 3–4 lb on worm, crab or shellfish fished at 20–50 yards. Winter fishing is mainly whiting, pout, dabs (which relish tiny pieces of aged squid) and a rare cod or two.

At **Hill Head** the beach becomes very shallow and the tide goes out a long way by local standards. It's a very popular ground for rag, silvers, lug and shellfish, but the fishing is nothing special.

Flounder sport can be quite good in autumn and winter, and an onshore blow and flooding spring tide can combine to produce bass. The most popular spot is the wall at the west side of **Titchfield Haven**, perhaps because you can actually fish from your car! There are worthwhile cod to be had from here in the good years.

Access becomes more difficult from here on, with a slog along the beach. A few small stingray are caught on calm summer evenings and nights, mainly on king rag or peeler crab. A night high tide in September or October can produce decent thornbacks to 10 lb or so, mainly to long casters or to 'backing up' tactics.

The next good spot is **Solent Breezes**, attained by driving down a rough track. Mainly noted for flounders, it has a deserved reputation for early season bass, with the first fish showing in February – mainly school fish to 4 lb or so. Best results come on spring tides, fishing three hours each side of high tide. Later in the season, weed can be pretty dreadful.

The **River Hamble** itself contains a king's ransom in yachts and cruisers, along with a thriving population of silver eels, flounders, bass and mullet. The mullet run right up to Botley

Top matchman Ian Golds with a winter cod caught from Hayling Island beach with the flooding tide.

From **Hamble Common** along to **Weston Shore** is one of the most popular of match venues. It is popular because of its consistency and generally even nature, for apart from the occasional decent plaice at Hamble sport consists almost entirely of flounders, school bass, mullet and silver eels. Best results come in October—January, and again in April, when the flounders return from spawning. Ragworm is generally the best bait and there is seldom a need for long casting — 80 yards or less will find fish. Daylight spring tides are best, two to three hours each side of high water.

Southampton Docks, sadly, are closed to anglers, and much of the eastern side is occupied by the massive Esso oil refinery. There is some fair flounder fishing from **Hythe Pier**, but general access does not resume until Calshot Spit. There is deep water at the extremity of **Calshot**, but mostly this is shallow ground running west to Calshot Foreshore Country Park. The fish are typical of the Solent: silver eels and bass in summer, flounders in winter, pout by night.

Access becomes increasingly difficult along this coastline as the sea-front roads disappear and privately-owned agricultural land tends to border the sea. The next easy point of call is at **Lepe**, home of excellent ragworm beds and some top-line winter flounder fishing. Best fish exceed 2 lb and there is a real chance of cod at night. Summer fishing tends to be a bit patchy, mainly eels and small fish, but with a few big soles and sometimes intruders like thornback ray on night tides.

Past the Beaulieu River lies **Park Shore**, which is reached by taking the small signposted turning some three-quarters of a mile west of St Leonards Grange. There is a car parking area followed by a modest and very pleasant walk to the sea. Park Shore is privately owned by the Montague Estate, and day or annual fishing permits are available from the John Montague Centre at Beaulieu. Telephone (0590) 612345 for current prices and details.

Park Shore at one time produced beach-caught tope, and they remain a possibility. However, it is best known for some very good smoothhound and stingray fishing. The smoothies run to 15 lb or more and can be plentiful on the right tide, whilst the stingray could conceivably go well over 50 lb. You need a warm, settled spell in the June—August period, and to fish an evening high tide, ideally in a flat calm. Best baits are peeler crab for the smoothies and king ragworm for the rays — set up your reel for a check run and wait for action. If the smoothhounds are in, you will very soon know about it, but if not, there is always the chance of a stinger. Other species to show are bass, eels and flatties, including the occasional very big sole, and in winter a cod.

At **Sowley Sedge**, to the west, the fishing is very similar except that you really need a small to medium neap tide – Sowley disappears underwater on springs. This is another private beach, but anglers are tolerated if they don't cause a nuisance. Find a parking space by Sowley Pond and walk down the lane to the beach. The shore-caught record stingray of 51 lb 4 oz came from Sowley.

For the moment, I will pass by the saltmarshes around Lymington (these are dealt with on pages 90–93), and move on to **Hurst Beach**, which is a long shingle spit guarding the western entrance to the Solent. Its strategic importance is such that Henry VIII built a castle there which has periodically been reinforced at times of war. To anglers, it is probably the best mark in Hampshire. From Keyhaven, a tiny lane to a footbridge crossing the back channel saves a slog along the beach – even so it is over a mile to the Castle, hard going over the shifting pebbles.

Round the corner from the Castle are the 'back sandbars', highly popular with local match anglers because of their great consistency. Fish one hour before to three hours after high water for dabs, flounders, some plaice and sole, bass, pout, bream, and cod in winter.

Garfish sometimes shoal in huge numbers off the Castle in late summer and shallow-set float gear can provide great daytime sport. The vicinity of the Castle is also a popular area for spinning, with most anglers favouring a Toby, krill, or similar self-weighted wobbling spoon in silver or silver-blue. It's a pleasant way to spend a long summer evening, wandering the Shingle Bank and Castle with spinning gear, and productive not only of mackerel, but sometimes gars, scad, pollack, bass, and in recent seasons occasional coalfish.

There is deep water off the Castle, and big baits may give tremendous fish, mainly bass, cod or conger. The **Shingle Bank** itself is swept by a very fierce tide on the flood, nearly always well laden with weed. You should aim to start fishing around high water on a neap tide and fish the ebb down. This is the best cod beach in the county for big fish, with double-figure specimens regularly taken and best individuals going over 20 lb. With the Needles cod marks only four or five miles away there has always got to be the chance of a 30 or 40 lb jumbo wandering inshore one fine rough night . . .

Standard codding tactics pay off, with rag, lug, peeler crab or livebaits successful. Long casting is seldom necessary – sometimes a 50-yard lob will catch, usually 70–100 yards is enough.

Summer fishing can be good, too, with lots of black bream to 1 lb or so, pout, bass, smoothhound, thornback ray (sadly much reduced in recent years), dogfish and some huge soles. Unpredictable and often disappointing, on the right night you will have a session that you won't quickly forget.

From Hurst westwards is the wide sweep of Christchurch Bay, basically a shingle beach backed by low, crumbling earth cliffs, that runs from Milford-on-Sea down to Barton-on-Sea, where the beach becomes more sandy, and thence to Chewton Bunny and finally to the Dorset border. Off the B3058, which runs from Milford to Barton, lies firstly **Hordle Cliff** and secondly **Taddiford**.

This whole stretch fishes best from May through to October or November. Bass, eels, pout, flounders and plaice are all taken regularly, but the two species most anglers target on are small-eyed rays and soles. Both can be caught throughout this length, but in general the best ray sport comes at **Hordle** and **Milford**, the most soles at **Taddiford**, and the biggest soles at **Barton**.

You need reasonably calm seas, a spring tide high about three or four hours after dark, and then fish four hours up and two hours back. Weed is sometimes a major problem, but quite often it forms a thick band close to the beach, and if it is calm enough to keep your line clear of the breakers you can fish without major problems. Tactics are clear cut. For the soles, you need a two- or three-hook paternoster armed with hooks between size 4 and 1, baited with ragworm or lug, with the fish seldom more than 60 yards out and often much closer.

The rays are primarily fish eaters, and for these you need either very fresh killed or frozen sandeel, or a fillet of pout caught on a second rod, and to blast your tackle 100 yards plus. That's not a firm figure – at Milford there is an offshore sandbar, which, like most sandbars, shifts according to wind and tide. You can see where it is from the cliff top by watching waves breaking over it at low tide. The rays seem to work the edges of the bar, and if you cannot reach the seaward side where most are caught, you are likely better off dropping on the inward edge rather than on top of it.

Harbours and marshes – Chichester, Langstone, Portsmouth and Lymington/Pennington/Keyhaven

THERE is as much fishing around the harbours and marshes of Hampshire as there is in or outside the Solent, even though much of Portsmouth harbour is restricted due to commercial or military

Huge packs of smoothhound run the Solent. Be in the right place at the right time and you too can catch fish like this!

dock establishments. All are important nursery areas for immature bass and are therefore heavily gill-netted. This has also had a serious adverse effect on the mullet population — mainly thick-lips and golden-greys — although there are still enough left to produce hair-tearing frustration.

Masses of silver eels are taken from May to September, and there is very good flounder fishing, mainly for fish from 12 oz to 1½ lb. When the year classes are right, much bigger fish are taken — I saw one match angler weigh in three flounders and a mullet of about 1½ lb a few years back for a huge total weight of 9 lb 12 oz, and yet big flounders were so common that year that to the best of my knowledge no one bothered to weigh them individually. There are a few authentic 4-pounders on record, but generally anything over 2½ lb is exceptional.

As far as the shore angler is concerned, the best flounder fishing is in April, then from October to the end of January. The biggest catches come when the sea is calm and crystal clear, but these conditions also produce the most blanks. An onshore blow producing a definite lop on the sea and plenty of colour in the water will nearly always get a few flounders feeding, but will rarely yield a huge bag. In the harbours, daylight tides are most consistent for the winter flounders; night tides are patchy and in some places utterly useless.

The harbours present a real problem to the visiting angler, and a bigger one to me as a writer endeavouring to advise you. There is, in the great majority of places, nothing but mud except for two or at best two and a half hours each side of high tide. On a small neap tide, there is not even water for that long and even at high tide it may be too shallow for fish to move in with confidence unless the water is coloured.

The key to fishing the harbours is the myriad small creeks or leats that criss-cross the mud — they may be only a few feet across and only a foot or two deeper than the surrounding mud flats, but they are the routes the flounders (and other fish) use on and off their rich feeding grounds, and they are where they feel secure.

Thus an error in position on the beach of a dozen feet may make the difference between a good session and one or two fish snared as they spread over the mud at high water. Local experts tend not to cast very far, but they cast very accurately. And so, it is essential to inspect the area at low tide in order to get the most out of your brief four hours' fishing. Some creeks produce better than others, but variations occur from season to season. I find it fascinating and challenging fishing, and the marshes have a special beauty on a crisp winter dawn, but it is not easy for the transient angler to build up the understanding needed for constant success. Unless you are prepared to put in a lot of time I would direct you to the accessible and more straightforward fishing in Southampton Water, from Weston to Hamble Common.

The mullet are another tricky proposition. When the water is reasonably deep, and where man is accepted as part of the waterside scene, they are perfectly catchable. Southampton's Ocean Village, Portsmouth's Camber Docks and any of the many marinas have resident mullet well used to feeding on bread or other scraps. In the Camber, where there is a fish market, they are more accustomed to eat fish.

However, the mullet of the shallow mudflats, though painfully obvious in the clear water, are very difficult indeed. As far as I can see, they eat mud, and let their tough digestions sort out the algal or other microscopic food content. A sudden movement on shore or in the water spooks the whole shoal and it takes a long time to wean them on to the sort of bait that will conceal a hook.

Boat fishing tactics

THERE is such a wide range of boat fishing available from Hampshire ports and the many public slipways that it is all too easy to find yourself going to sea with half a dozen different rods − I do it all the time! However, let me try instead to rationalise the minimum gear you will need effectively to deal with most of the situations you will encounter.

For the big cod off the **Needles** or south of the **Nab Tower**, for the conger and tope of **Dunnose Head** or St Catherine's Deeps, and for heavy bottom fishing, pirking on wrecks, or shark you will need a 50 lb class rod (with an overall length of between 7 and 8 feet) equipped with Aftco or Hopkins + Holloway roller rings.

No serious angler would consider fishing any of these productive marks without wire line − in the strong tidal flows of the Wight grounds this should at least double your catches when compared with nylon line. A tough reel in the 4/0 or 6/0 range is needed to cope with punishing conditions, and you can rely on Daiwa, Penn, Shakespeare or Shimano in the right size.

Wire should be 30 lb or 40 lb breaking strain; braids are easier to handle but tend to be expensive, whilst single-strand is more likely to kink − and thus be weakened − but does not fray. Good braids are T.W.L. or Marlinsteel, and the most readily available single-strand is Nicro. Quite a few tackle shops buy giant bulk spools of nickel-chrome wire and provide a 'fill your own reel' service to anglers at a very competitive price, and the wire is good stuff.

Uptiding has really taken off in Hampshire over recent years, and it is now the first choice method for many situations. If you buy a powerful rod capable of casting up to 8 oz for deeper water it will also double fairly well when fishing an artificial eel for pollack and in a number of conventional bottom fishing roles as well. Add a light uptider casting say 2−5 oz and it will also handle inshore plaice fishing, black bream and drifted sandeel for bass. Good reels for the job include ABU 7000 series and 9000, Shimano TLD 10 or 15, Daiwa PMF 55H or PMF 57H, or the LD30H and LD50H from the same stable.

If you prefer to have exactly the right rod for each job, you can perhaps add in a salmon spinning rod for plaice and bass fishing, a 30 lb class rod ringed for wire, 12 and 20 lb class rods for conventional bottom fishing and − should you wish to dinghy fish for flounders in the harbours − a 6- or 7-foot trout spinning rod.

Many of the techniques used off Hampshire are standard. For instance, codling, tope and smoothhounds will all generally best be sought uptiding with a running leger rig, respectively baited with lugworm, mackerel or silver eel, and peeler or hermit crab. Rather than deal at length with routine tactics I would like instead to consider those more specific to the area.

The best plaice marks are in Hayling Bay, off Eastney, and thence into the Solent. Usually the water will be from 10−30 feet deep, the seabed sand, shingle, shell, or mussel beds and the tide moderate to brisk throughout the productive times. Local experts favour a two-hook flowing trace incorporating a 2½ or 3-inch wobbling ice-fishing lure as an uptrace attractor. The tackle is cast at right angles to the boat and allowed to roll around with the tide until it comes to rest astern, when it is worked with a gentle sink and draw action. Bites are gentle, as a rule, and need to be allowed time to develop.

In some years the water temperature in early season is so low that the plaice are sluggish and disinterested in a moving bait. Although the basic end rig stays the same, hook lengths are reduced to 6 lb and hooks to a size 4 or 6, with a small bait, fished stationary except for occasional tweaks to stir up the sand.

Key water temperature seems to be about 7°C − you do not need a thermometer, water temperature is included on the Marinecall weather forecast on 0898 500457. Plaice can be fussy feeders and will leave a bait if they feel excess resistance from the rod-tip − light tackle is not only more fun but more successful.

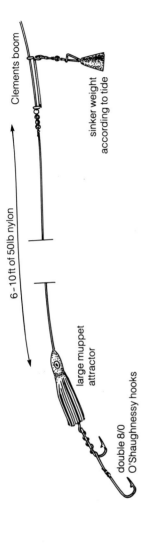

Figure 8 Heavy cod rig for Needles and Nab marks

Clements boom

sinker weight
according to tide

6–10ft of 50lb nylon

large muppet
attractor

double 8/0
O'Shaughnessy hooks

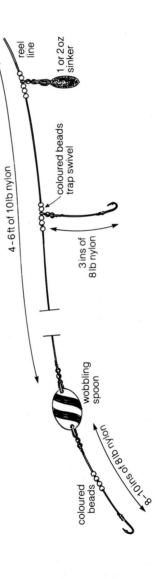

Figure 9 Plaice rig for boat fishing

reel line

1 or 2oz sinker

coloured beads
trap swivel

4–6ft of 10lb nylon

3ins of
8lb nylon

wobbling spoon

8–10ins of 8lb nylon

coloured beads

The legendary big cod of the Isle of Wight grounds are mainly caught on the well-proven wire line technique. A short 6–10-foot length of 40 lb nylon leader is attached to the wire line with an Albright knot, and the lead boom runs on this. An alternative to the Albright is to sheath the wire line in a one-inch length of telephone wire covering – you can uni-knot direct to this. The 6–12-foot flowing trace of 50 lb nylon carries 6/0 or 8/0 O'Shaughnessy hooks rigged Pennell style. A big muppet or a white spoon uptrace provides additional attraction to the double squid bait as it is carefully trotted back downtide, perhaps as much as 100 yards away when the tide is screaming through.

The initial bite can often be extremely gentle, and the timing of the strike is all important – wait until the bite is really going well or until the cod turns down tide with the bait before winding up tight and lifting into it. Remember it is very hard to be too late and very easy to be too early. Do not try to bully the fish to the boat – firm but controlled is the way to do it.

Dinghy fishing for flounders in the harbours is great fun and extremely productive. From April to early October the way to succeed is to fish a ragworm-baited spoon. The spoon itself should be from two and a half to four inches long, be made of metal, and the single kirbed size 2 hook must not revolve. The bend of the hook should be one and a half to two and a half inches behind the rear of the spoon blade. The spoon should be chrome or silver for general-purpose use, white for coloured water or low light and red for very clear water and bright sunshine.

Whether you opt to cast and retrieve the spoon, or whether you prefer to troll under very gentle oar power, it is essential that the spoon travels with the current – very few flounders take a spoon moving against the flow. There is no need for the spoon to fish very close to the bottom, for flounders detect them easily and will swim well off the seabed to intercept and take the bait. When casting the spoon, I have many times had bites when the spoon was a couple of feet from the dinghy, although the water was upwards of 20 feet deep. When a shoal of flounders is coming through, you can expect a bite every cast, and since it takes only 30 seconds or so to fish each cast out, that represents quick-fire action!

Guide to the boat marks

AS far as charter boat fishing is concerned, there are substantial fleets based at **Langstone** and **Lymington**, with smaller numbers operating out of **Portsmouth harbour** and **Keyhaven**. Boats

Bass, like this double-figure fish, roam the sandbanks and gullies of the western Solent. This fish was caught off Lymington

based at **Yarmouth**, on the Isle of Wight, will also pick up anglers from Lymington or Keyhaven without extra charge — outside the holiday season the Isle of Wight population is too small to provide regular employment for them.

So popular is the Solent as a boating area that there is no shortage of public slipways available to dinghy anglers, either free or for a very modest charge. Some dry out at low water springs, but generally they are good. It would take too long to list all the slips here, but you can readily get afloat at **Hayling Ferry** (east side), **Camber Docks, Portsmouth, Stokes Bay, Gosport** (follow signs for 'angling club'), **Calshot** and **Lymington** (west side, Bath Road car park). As the fishing tends to be better outside the Solent, most anglers prefer to launch at the extremities of the Isle of Wight to cut down on steaming time. All the above slips, except Calshot and Stokes, are in very sheltered waters and launching is possible in any weather that will permit safe fishing.

One of the most popular areas for Langstone and Portsmouth boats is actually over the border, in West Sussex. I include **Selsey** in this chapter because you are far more likely to fish it from Langstone than from the nearest Sussex port, Littlehampton. Langstone is not only nearer to Selsey, but the spring tides, when it fishes best, tend to take the boats down there in the morning and carry them home at the end of the day.

There is a good mix of ground off Selsey, from the very deep holes just off the **Pullar Buoy** to the shallow reefs of the **Inner Ledge**. There are some cracking black bream on the latter in May and June, but you need a skipper who really knows the ground. The first time I fished it was on a dropping tide, and as slack water approached dozens of lobster-pot markers began to surface, whilst more alarmingly, rocks began to make their appearance in the clear water. In fact the skipper knew exactly what he was doing and we exited on the flood tide with bream to nearly 4 lb — great fun.

There is wonderful tope fishing off the Pullar between late April and June, with recent specimens approaching 70 lb and very large numbers — hit a pack and it's quite possible to have a fish on every rod, and big ones at that.

In more moderate depths quality smoothhound fishing can be had on crab bait, with plenty of fish to 23 lb or so taken each season — generally, though, anything over 14 lb is a respectable specimen. As a rule, the shallower the water, the more effectively peeler crab performs. In deeper water, hermit crab is as good, and when lesser spotted dogfish are a nuisance, hardback shore crabs will keep them at bay.

The hard-running tope offer exceptional light tackle sport for the boat angler. This 35-pounder was hooked between Hayling Island and the border with Sussex

Thornback ray, small-eyed ray, conger, pout, wrasse, bass and occasional cod also feature in Selsey spring and summer catches. It is not fished so much in winter, when a sudden deterioration in the weather can leave a long slog home into a west or sou'west gale, but there are quality cod to be had on squid baits.

The sandy seabed of **Bracklesham Bay** to the west is good for autumn and winter whiting and a few cod, whilst smaller hooks can find dabs and plaice. Dogfish can be a menace here.

A variety of marks in this sector of East Wight waters are good for bream; common factors are shallow waters over chalky reef. The **Looe Gate**, off Selsey, the **Boulder Bank**, the **Hounds**, **Bullock Patch** and **Bembridge Ledge** are all well-known marks which produce great sport in season — May and June, sometimes July. A light tackle approach, balanced to the tidal conditions, is best. Bream can sometimes be very fussy about baits — one of my personal favourites is a blow lug/squid cocktail, but squid and cuttle strip, rag, lug and mackerel or herring strip all have their moments.

Hayling Bay has good inshore fishing for plaice and dabs — both are present all year round, but plaice are most plentiful March to May. The little gully just south of Church Rocks is good. Winter fishing sees plenty of small pout and whiting and a few cod on the same ground.

For the sake of the bass, presently under dreadful pressure from netsmen and commercial 'anglers', I am unwilling to reveal shoaling areas. One that everybody knows is **Langstone Run**, fished either from a drifting or an anchored dinghy with live sandeel on driftline gear. The bass tend to be under 4 lb, and although the occasional fish for family consumption is acceptable, most thinking anglers return them.

The mussel beds between the **West Winner** and the **Blocks** have been scraped close to destruction by trawlers, but in isolated pockets plaice to 4 lb and sometimes better can be had in spring.

Further offshore a number of popular marks are within reach of a seaworthy displacement dinghy in the right weather. **Dean Tail**, **New Grounds** and **Nab East** all give dabs, cod, pout and whiting in winter; rays, dogfish and smoothhounds in summer.

East of the buoys marking the end of the dredged channel and east and south of the **Nab Tower**, there are banks rising to within 50 feet or so of the surface.

Uptide tactics with crab bait yield good smoothhound and occasional thornback from May to July, with a decline in catches in August and September. Fresh mackerel bait will produce tope. Winter shows whiting and cod, some of the latter approaching

40 lb in good seasons. Although the **East Wight** has plenty of small and medium cod in boom years for the species, the normal pattern is for small numbers of fish in the 15−25 lb class. Best whiting can top 4 lb and in a good season 3 lb fish are not uncommon.

From **Culver Cliff** round to the west side of **Sandown Bay** there is good fishing for rays, mainly small-eyed, with some bass, small brill and turbot. The fish are found on inshore sandbanks that run south from the island shore, where they feed on big launce.

Further offshore the deep holes off **Dunnose Head** and in **St Catherine's Deeps** offer good conger to 40 lb or so, together with bull huss, best fishing being in late summer and autumn. Sometimes pack tope gather off 'St Cath's' in great numbers and 60 or more fish in a session is perfectly possible.

Big tidal overfalls build up along this stretch, and even in calm conditions spectacular shows of white water can be seen. There are usually plenty of mackerel and on the right day good pollack and bass can be taken on artificial sandeels or on live eels or small whole mackerel. First light is a good time, but these are dangerous waters and need to be respected.

Charter boats tend to fish the Solent itself only when adverse weather conditions rule out more distant marks. Although the Solent is sheltered, a combination of strong tides and shallow water can mean a short, ugly sea developing in a very short time. There are many restrictions on anchoring and fishing and in particular the approaches to Southampton Water are constantly used by very large and heavily laden vessels which have no sea space to manoeuvre around angling dinghies. It is essential to get an up-to-date chart and to obey the current regulations.

You can enjoy useful bass fishing through much of the Solent, despite the gill-netters. The best way to catch small to medium bass is by drifting with live sandeels. You can find shoaling fish by watching the sea birds work, especially the delicate and beautiful terns, which have the ability consistently to locate bass. The indiscriminate gulls will flock over mackerel or anything else, including sewage. Large bass tend to come from deeper water and mainly take big baits of fresh mackerel, cuttlefish or squid.

There is deep water off **Fort Gilkicker** which produces a variety of species but is especially good for winter cod. **Stokes Bay** has more cod, with whiting, pout and flatties. Opposite Stokes lies the **Mother Bank** and north-west of that is **Ryde Middle**. These yield a few rays in summer and cod, pout and whiting in autumn and winter.

The shallow ground off **Lee-on-Solent** often has some lively plaice fishing from April through to autumn. The fish tend to move around and it can pay to drift the ground until a concentration is found and then anchor uptide of them. Part of the **Bramble Bank** dries at low-water springs, but the edges of the Bank can give good bags of smoothhound to crab bait, especially on evening tides.

The **West Solent** has good summer fishing for smoothies, stingray and bass. Weed is often a major problem so it is better to fish neap tides, with night fishing very much better than daylight. There are lots of drop-offs where the prehistoric **Solent River** had its bed and you should aim to fish these until last light, when it is prudent to move out of harm's way, close inshore off **Thorness Bay**, **Salt Mead**, **Sowley** or **Park Shore**. Downtide casting with crab or ragworm will score.

Autumn and winter offer some respectable fishing for cod and whiting, but the best results come on the famed **Needles** marks. However, be warned, the tides in the West Solent, and especially off Hurst, can be extremely strong and potentially dangerous.

The **Shingles Bank** has some reasonable bass fishing on live sandeel or trolled artificials, and there is good sport to be had uptiding for small-eyed rays, thornbacks and occasionally others. There is better fishing still on the spectacular sandbanks of **Freshwater Reef**, where bass, brill, turbot and all the rays regularly feature. Far and away the most successful tactic is uptiding, and some local skippers have this down to a fine art. A long, flowing trace is used, of 18–20 lb nylon with a small hook − size 1 or 2 O'Shaughnessy or Uptide Extra. A small piece of fresh mackerel is the bait, and results can be very good. Small-eyeds can exceed 12 lb; turbot tend to be small, but occasionally run into the teens of pounds.

Needles cod are big; usually 18–25 lb, but plenty of 'thirties' and one or two 'forties' are taken each season. If you don't use wire line and big baits of two *calimari* squid, you are unlikely to catch any! Even when you do things right, three or four fish in the boat represents a reasonable return. Sharing the same ground and season are big whiting, plenty of small/medium conger, a few big pollack, occasional ling and countless pout and dogfish. Spurdog can be plentiful, especially on the deeper marks.

There are many wrecks off the Hampshire coast, but the generally rather shallow water means that most of the productive ones lie 20 miles or more out. There is good pollack sport for fish to 15 lb or so on **West Wight** wrecks in March and April. They move on to **East Wight** hulks from May, and are joined by cod for

Southampton Water offers a wide variety of angling, especially for the small-boat angler. Here we see England international Ted Entwistle and his wife with a stingray caught close to Calshot

a few short weeks. In August and September it becomes increasingly necessary to travel long distances for the best results, and ling and conger begin to dominate catches. There has been little winter wrecking done locally, but test fishing has not produced any startling results at present.

Hampshire is the number one spot in the country for thresher shark, the great majority of this scarce species having come between **Selsey** and **St Catherine's**, including the record of 323 lb and a number of 250 lb plus fish. Specimens estimated at over 500 lb are sighted most years.

There was at one time superb porbeagle fishing, but far too many big fish were killed by anglers and many are now taken by French longliners on their 12-mile lines. You can still have good results if you hit a shoal, but there are more blanks than enough and the average size of fish has now settled in the 80–140 lb range. Still, on a 30 lb class outfit fish like that can give tremendous sport . . .

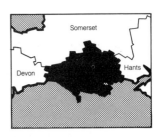

Chris Clark

DORSET

DORSET offers some exciting fishing, says
Lymington-based Chris Clark, another member of
the England squad. He is also a very successful
local match angler.

A DRAMATIC AND VARIED COASTLINE

THE Dorset coastline offers the sea angler perhaps the most varied sea fishing around Great Britain. A brave statement, but the shoreline can claim several unique features.

Geographically it is ideally situated, with its western fringe feeling the benefits of the warm Gulf Stream, which often brings many rare species close inshore during the long summer months, while it is close enough to the North Sea to take full advantage of migrating cod and whiting throughout the colder winter months.

Because of South Coast trade links with the rest of the world, wrecks of all kinds litter the seabed, making a safe refuge for many species which often grow to record-breaking proportions.

Lying mid-way along the English Channel, the coastline varies from the popular holiday resorts of Poole and Bournemouth to the massive landslips that occur from the high fossil-bearing cliffs just east of Lyme Regis.

Tucked in between these two extremities are several very interesting features, which offer every type of sea angling imaginable. These include Poole harbour, which is one of the largest natural harbours in the world, the often hostile cliffs of Purbeck, the Isle of Portland, which has a beauty all of its own, to the 18-mile strip of shingle which makes up the famous Chesil Beach.

The geology which has created this beautiful coastline has left many strange features, such as Old Harry rock, Durdle Door and the unique Lulworth Cove, where the sea has made slow advances over the years and eaten out the soft limestone cliffs, leaving the harder rocks, which has resulted in a series of picturesque coves, arches and fairy-tale rock formations.

The county has four distinct seasons as far as fishing is concerned, but there are many overlaps which vary from year to year depending on weather conditions. Apart from the seasons, fish movement is also governed by the availability of food, although pouting, dabs and dogfish seem to be ever present.

Plaice are the first species to make their presence felt, moving inshore in large numbers from March onwards, especially in the west of the region, where catches peak towards the end of June. Good-size plaice also turn up in fair numbers in Bournemouth Bay, although catches are mainly restricted to boat anglers drifting a few hundred yards offshore.

The first mackerel shoals start to appear towards the end of April with Chesil Beach and Lyme Bay the number one target areas. Their numbers slowly build up as the summer progresses and they spread throughout the region. 'Old green bones', the garfish, with their long snout-like beaks arrive just before the mackerel, which are in turn quickly followed by many larger predatory species such as conger, tope, rays and even a fair number of sharks.

From mid-June onwards three other species join the rapidly increasing number of summer fish – smoothhound, the shy and somewhat elusive mullet and the silver flanked bass, which is without question the king of all the sea fish. Smoothhound catches are mainly restricted to venues towards the western end of Dorset with Chesil Beach certainly turning out some hefty specimens. The shy mullet, on the other hand, filter into the many creeks and harbours throughout the area as well as turning up at some of the more rocky locations, where they feed off maggots washed out of decaying seaweed left along the high-tide line. Big bass can turn up anywhere in the region with particular emphasis on kelp-covered rocks and tide races.

Towards the end of July and early August, with the sea temperature rapidly increasing, there's an explosion of activity with many species starting to make their presence felt. These would include the nocturnal sole, which are particularly active towards Dorset's eastern fringe, while wrasse, bream and pollack show in numbers around rocky locations.

The autumn sees a rush of activity during the cross-over period, with many summer species slowly melting away, while the winter's arrival of cod, whiting, flounders, conger and specimen-size wrasse really gets into full swing.

The winter months between November and January are productive with prime-conditioned flounders feeding in many backwater areas, while whiting, cod and dabs appear in numbers from both boat marks and along Chesil Beach.

Dorset's fishing potential is controlled very much by the weather. The cold frosty days of January, when the wind is mainly from a northerly direction, are ideal for flounder fishing, while on the other hand a good south-westerly switches the cod into a feeding frenzy. April and early May are normally pretty settled months with just a light south-westerly air stream resulting in near perfect conditions for the boat angler to try deep-water wrecking trips or the shore angler to bait his hook for plaice.

The strength of the wind always seems to increase towards the end of May with surf beaches certainly coming into their own during this period. During the long summer months, when beaches become packed with holidaymakers, anglers arm themselves with light float tackle and head for the rocks, particularly during long, settled periods of weather.

The whole coastline is normally lashed by gales during the autumn equinox which stirs many fish into life, although the turbulent seas rip tons of seaweed from the seabed, which quickly clog anglers' lines. As winter approaches winds swing east and this brings the cod.

There's minimum tidal movement along the Dorset coast, which has the lowest rise and fall in the country. This is a plus factor for the beach angler, who can fish the same spot virtually all day without being forced to move by the tide. However, the lack of tidal movement is a bait digger's nightmare, with only a small expanse of beach becoming exposed at low water.

Surprisingly, many areas of the coastline are swept by exceptionally strong currents, particularly around Portland, which is washed by a very strong tidal race. These strong currents churn up the seabed, resulting in a constant supply of rich food for fish to feed on.

The Dorset coast can be divided into five distinct areas. The first area starts on the county's eastern fringe and takes in all of Poole Bay. The second region extensively covers Poole harbour, while the next region deals with the whole of the Purbeck coast. The Isle of Portland and Weymouth is dealt with together, while the final area covers the mighty Chesil Beach and sweeping Lyme Bay.

Tackling the Dorset shoreline

CHOOSING the right gear to tackle the Dorset coastline can cause a few headaches, since several complete outfits are needed to cope with all the varying angling situations.

Although one all-purpose rod would cover most needs, in real terms five different rods would be more appropriate to cope with so many varying venues and specialised fishing techniques. Care is also needed when choosing beachcasters, as distance casting is essential from a number of locations. My own personal preference for general beach work is a Zziplex 250M, a rod well capable of thumping baits out in excess of 150 yards while at the same time having a very sensitive tip to show up the bites.

A lightweight beachcaster will also come into its own when flounder fishing in Poole harbour or the Fleet, which runs behind

Chesil Beach. A soft, all-through action rod would be suitable for this type of fishing and I favour the Zziplex NG2.

For rough ground conger and wrasse fishing a very strong pole is needed. Give a hefty conger an inch with a soft all-through action rod and you are asking to loose it. Here I would go for the Quatra, another rod from the Zziplex stable. However, I would suggest cutting off the top three inches to beef it up. This rod is certainly more than adequate to cope with any conger likely to be encountered from the beach.

An 11 foot carp rod is certainly an essential item, for during the warm summer months this rod can be used for light line float fishing for wrasse, mullet, mackerel, garfish and pollack. A good-quality carp rod will also double up as a spinning rod, for there are many rocky outcrops where pollack can be taken on Red Gills or small spinners.

A fly rod also comes into its own when the shy Purbeck mullet are on the hit list. In such cases hooks are baited with maggots and cast towards the mullet as they move close to the shoreline. No need to spend a fortune on this pole, but try to pick out one that is fairly robust.

Reels are very much a personal preference, but they do fall into several categories. For general beach fishing you won't go far wrong with a Daiwa Millionaire 6HM or the new Shimano Triton Speed Master, multiplier reels more than capable of tackling the everyday rigours of both sand and shingle beaches. If I had to choose between the two then the Speed Master would just have the edge, mainly because of its fast retrieve, which is an advantage when fishing over roughish ground. Assuming that a 50 lb shock leader is used, then 12 lb to 15 lb mainline is more than sufficient to cope with all but rocky marks along the Dorset coast.

Heavy-duty reels are required if you intend fishing from the many rock marks for wrasse, pollack and conger. The sturdy ABU 7000 multiplier takes some beating here. Because of the rough terrain, 30 lb line fished straight through is preferable, although power casting is a non-starter unless a leader is used.

There are numerous small, freshwater fixed-spool reels on the market, many capable of handling sea angling jobs. Personally, I would plump for the Shakespeare Omni 050. Loaded with 5 lb or 6 lb line it certainly lets wrasse, pollack and garfish show off their full fighting qualities.

The centre-pin fly reel used for mullet is a specialised item, so I wouldn't advise sea anglers going over the top when buying a reel which is often only used a few times a year. A DAM Quickfly 90 is quite adequate.

A wide range of leads are needed to cope with various fishing situations you are likely to be faced with — these can range from quiet back-waters to fierce tidal races. In general, 4 oz to 5 oz plain bomb leads and Breakaway-type grip sinkers will cope with most situations, although smaller weights can often be beneficial, especially when flounder or bass fishing in quiet harbour locations.

Snaggy rock marks call for something special, and many anglers use throwaway spark plugs or strips of old lead to save on costly sinkers. In my book this is often a false economy since this type of lead weight is easily snagged and fish are lost. Try a 3 oz or 4 oz flat shape moulded sinker used in conjunction with a Lead Lift to cut down on foul-ups.

There's one item of gear that's a must when fishing in Dorset — a good landing or drop net. Many of the better wrasse marks can only be fished from lofty ledges, making a drop net a necessity to both land and return fish. A good, stout, wide landing net is also crucial for both light line spinning and float fishing. Swinging a 5 lb fish in on light line is a non-starter.

Terminal tackle is pretty standard with a three-hook paternoster-type rig being the basic outfit cast from many beaches, although, like most areas, there are a few specialities which definitely seem to increase the catch rate. Chesil Beach is a prime example, where the long see-saw-type 'wishbone' rig really sorts out both the flatties and cod when the tide is running at its peak.

Wrasse and conger rigs also call for something special with a rotten bottom incorporated in both cases. My normal conger rig is a fairly simple affair with the snood length made from 100 lb nylon rather than wire. I also steer away from the running leger system, preferring a fixed link. Wrasse rigs also need to be kept simple, so that snags are minimal. Wrasse often run big along the Dorset coast so don't be frightened to increase hook size. Use 4/0 or 6/0 when baiting with big crabs.

Float rigs will vary tremendously depending on water depth and the expected species. However, I normally find that a sliding float is ideal for the many deep-water marks that hold wrasse. I personally settle for the cigar-shaped Drennan No. 4, which will cope with most situations. I also try to keep an even spread of shot below the float rather than just a single 1 oz bomb-type sinker.

Using the correct bait is the secret to catching fish and there is no substitute for a good supply of quality bait. Dorset, like most other counties, does offer a fair range of baits for those collectors prepared to make the effort.

Starting in the east, sandeels can be collected at Mudeford,

Figure 10 Chesil Beach 'wishbone' rig

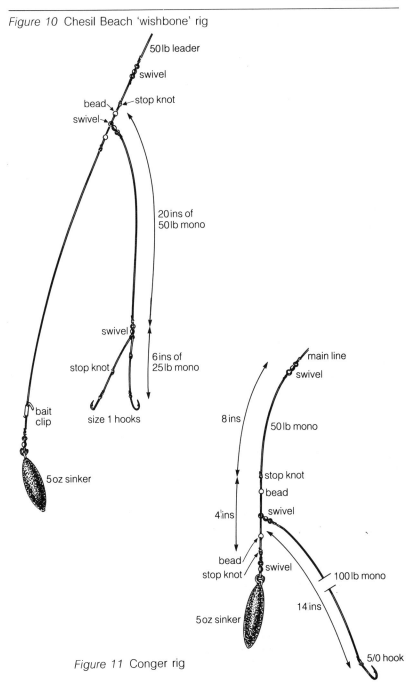

Figure 11 Conger rig

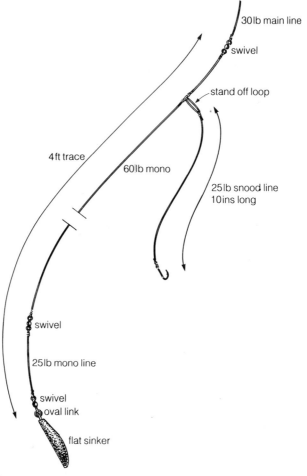

30lb main line

swivel

stand off loop

4ft trace

60lb mono

25lb snood line
10ins long

swivel

25lb mono line

swivel

oval link

flat sinker

Figure 12 Wrasse rig

near the entrance to Christchurch harbour, throughout the summer months, while lugworm can also be dug from Mudeford beach on big spring tides. Harbour rag can be dug in Christchurch harbour, where peeler crabs can also be found during the warmer months. There is little bait to be found along Bournemouth beach with the exception of mussels from the groynes, and slipper limpets which get washed up during stormy periods.

Poole harbour is a bait digger's paradise, offering both lugworm and ragworm in large numbers. Small harbour ragworm and white rag can also be found, but they are not so prolific. There's also peeler crab, hermit crab and shellfish. During the summer months both sandeel and fresh mackerel can be bought from the fishing boats moored alongside Poole quay.

Studland beach, just to the west of the harbour entrance, holds some good-size lug on spring tides, along with occasional white rag. A limited number of razorfish can also be collected on exceptionally low spring tides. Sandeels are far more plentiful and can be found in the sand just above the low-water mark, especially on night tides.

Moving west, Swanage beach holds limited amounts of small lug on low-water springs, but bait digging is frowned upon during the holiday months. Small crabs and shellfish can be collected from the western end of the bay near the pier, and good numbers of prawns and shrimps can also be taken from this area with a push net.

The coastline between Swanage and Weymouth, which includes the Purbeck coast, offers very little in the way of bait with the exception of small shore crabs, rock limpets, sea slaters and seaweed fly maggots, which can be found in the decaying seaweed along the high-tide mark, especially at Kimmeridge, Chapman's Pool and Mupe Bay.

A variety of baits can be collected in the Weymouth area. Preston beach can be dug for small lug and white rag on big tides along with a variety of shellfish, including razorfish during stormy periods. Weymouth harbour is the home of a fair head of shore crabs, with peelers found in its higher reaches.

Lugworm can be dug around the Weymouth end of the Fleet, along with small white rag and the odd king ragworm. Peeler crab can also be collected along the northern side of the Fleet. Portland harbour, directly opposite the Fleet, holds lugworm and good-size white rag on big spring tides.

Very little bait is available around Portland with the exception of rock limpets and sea slaters. Prawns and velvet swimming crabs can be caught in drop nets. There is a shellfish centre in Portland where both crabs and various shellfish can be bought.

The 18 miles of shingle which form Chesil Beach is completely devoid of bait. The tide never leaves the shingle beach. However, mackerel can be feathered during the season along the entire bank.

On Dorset's western fringe, bait is again pretty scarce, but a few small lugworm can be found between Charmouth and Lyme Regis, particularly on big tides, but don't expect a bucketful. Peeler crab are a possibility from the rocks just west of Charmouth and around Lyme Regis.

Shore fishing spots along the Dorset coast

SHALLOW-water beaches sweep along the whole of Poole Bay, which includes Christchurch, Bournemouth and, of course, Poole Bay itself, with the only respite being the small entrance to Christchurch harbour and the rocky outcrop at Hengistbury Head.

Looking towards Dorset's extreme eastern fringe **Highcliffe** is certainly worthy of mention. The nocturnal sole are active feeders between September and November with specimens up to 3 lb taken in recent years. Ragworm is the killer bait. Pouting also show in fair numbers throughout the autumn months along with whiting and the odd codling. A few school bass normally put in an appearance between May and September, while a few small flounders seem to be forever present. In recent years a few very long groynes have been constructed that are wide enough to fish from. These vantage points offer mackerel and small ray throughout the summer months.

Friars Cliff, next door to Highcliffe, is a match angler's dream during the autumn months, when plump pouting show in large numbers, mainly on night tides. All baits seem to take their toll, although in my book peeler crab and ragworm come out on top. A few hefty cod are also often recorded during the winter months along with whiting, rockling and few flatfish. Bass during the summer on freelined sandeel bait.

The shy and often elusive mullet appear in numbers throughout **Christchurch harbour** during the warm summer months, but anglers should note that a permit is required to fish all but the very lower reaches of the harbour. Small bass, eels and flounders feed during the summer and autumn months.

During strong south-westerly gales **Mudeford Spit**, which faces east, can offer some excellent sport with bass throughout the summer months, while hefty cod are the target species during winter. There's a fair tide race in the harbour entrance, where freelined sandeels take many bass. Cod can turn up anywhere along the spit, although the favoured areas are near the middle section, where lugworm or peeler crab fished on a night tide can work wonders. Flounders are plentiful throughout on both night and day tides, while some good-size plaice show during summer and pouting around autumn. The bottom is mainly sandy, but towards **Hengistbury Head** a few rocky outcrops appear which hold small wrasse during the warm summer months. Bait-robbing shore crabs can strip hooks quickly during settled weather.

During winter the only access to the spit involves a mile-long hike from the main car park at Hengistbury Head, although a ferry service operates throughout the summer months from Mudeford quay.

The ground around Hengistbury Head offers varied angling, with perhaps the groyne, which sticks out a 100 yards or so from the very point of the headland, the best bet throughout the summer months. Forget your heavy-duty beach rod here and go armed with a light spinning rod and some float tackle. Target species will be mackerel, garfish, pollack, wrasse, scad and some good-size bass. Best of the fishing occurs on the outermost tip of the groyne, which is swept by a strong tide race on the flood. Just flip a float rig baited with a fresh sandeel out a few yards and let the tide do the rest. Sport during early morning can be hectic.

The water off the end of the groyne is not deep, but the odd conger does still turn up on night tides, especially in the autumn. Fresh mackerel is the deadly bait. The stretch of beach running 200 to 300 yards west of the groyne can also be productive during the summer, with wrasse feeding on day tides and good-size sole, pouting and a few gurnard on night tides. Fish ragworm here.

The slightly shelving shingle beach at **Double Dykes** is a popular haunt with anglers from June through to December. Small turbot, plaice, flounders, bass and sole feed in summer with cod and whiting during winter. Night tides sort out the better fish, especially the sole and cod. Top baits include sandeel, lugworm and small strips of fresh mackerel. A flood tide topping out around midnight offers the best prospects.

Southbourne's sandy beach offers plenty of variety during autumn with night tides being the prime periods. Lugworm and ragworm will tempt sole, bass, plaice, flounders, cod, pouting and whiting, while a few good-size small-eyed ray are often taken on sandeels. The sole feed very close inshore, although as a rule distance casters will take the better catches of other species.

Bournemouth pier is a noted all-year flatfish mark. A few big plaice are caught every season on both ragworm and lugworm baits. Mackerel, scad and lively garfish visit the end of the pier and can be taken on light float tackle. Sizeable mullet and pollack lurk around the pier piles. **Boscombe pier** provides far better sport, although the structure is in urgent need of repair. When fishing is permitted many fish are taken, including dabs, flounders, plaice and pouting, with whiting the dominant species. A few brill also come to net. At the present time angling is severely restricted because of the condition of the pier.

Bournemouth beach, lying between the two piers, is worth fishing between January and March for small flounders during night tides. Dabs, pouting, rockling, whiting and the odd codling are also on the cards, with lugworm and ragworm taking most fish. The beach is a popular bathing area, so sport is restricted throughout the summer months. Fish at night for sole and pouting, but caution should be exercised when handling fish taken from this beach as weevers do appear in numbers.

Sandbanks is another busy holiday area, again where sport is restricted to the winter months for flounders, pouting, whiting and bass. A young flood tide is certainly a plus factor with worm baits again catching the fish. During early spring a few good-size plaice are on the cards.

Poole harbour is one of the major angling hotspots along the South Coast. Because of the harbour's geography, along with its many islands, many sheltered shore-fishing venues can be found even in the most severe weather conditions. The shallow waters around the harbour warm rapidly, providing a huge nursery area for small bass, mullet and flatfish. Recently sailboarders use the favourite flounder marks and conflicts seem inevitable. Also, shore crabs can be downright pests.

Looking at Poole harbour in more detail, and working in an anti-clockwise direction, we start at the **harbour entrance**, where the chain ferry links with the Studland shore. Strong tides rushing through this narrow gap have gouged out a relatively deep channel, where bass roam throughout the summer and autumn months. Small spinners or float-fished sandeel account for a number of fish ranging from schoolies through to double-figure fish.

The **Evening Hill** stretch of the harbour is prime flounder country during winter with fishing peaking early January. This is a shallow-water mark with the best sport occurring two hours either side of high water on both night and day tides. Bait and access are simple – a road runs parallel with the venue. Ragworm outfishes all other baits here.

Baiter Point is, without question, the most popular angling mark within the harbour. Alas, sailboarders also find it attractive! Another shallow venue, it offers sport from September through to January with specimen-size flounders. Again, a high-water venue, with ragworm taking many fish, although peeler crab is also effective during the autumn period. Daylight fishing will produce flatfish, although eels and small bass feed at night.

Another easy venue to fish is **Poole Quay** with its deep water right under the rod top. Inquisitive trippers can be a 'pain' during summer, so fish early morning or at night. Night tides bring flatties, eels, pouting, whiting and pollack, while those early

The Cobb, Lyme Regis, is an ideal place for light tackle fishing

morning trips offer bonus mullet, especially if grain ships are unloading their cargo next to the quay.

A new spur road has opened up a large area of **Holes Bay**, which was completely inaccessible to the beach angler in the past. Winter brings big flounder from the deep-water channel that runs close to this new road. Ragworm is again the top bait, while daytime fishing on a flood tide seems to be most fruitful. Light weight beach outfits or spoon tackle works in this area.

Two more good flounder marks are **Hamworthy** and **Rockley Sands**, and throughout the autumn there's the chance of the occasional eel, plaice and small bass. Fish ragworm and peeler crab baits over a flooding tide. Hamworthy is the spot for the larger flounders, while Rockley Sands has a reputation for yielding greater numbers.

There are numerous flattie marks dotted around the **Arne** peninsula, which juts out from the western side of the harbour. **Shipstal Point**, near the entrance to the Wych Channel, is one such mark that's worthy of a mention. During summer eels and small bass can be taken in numbers, but as autumn arrives flounders appear to specimen size. This is another high-water mark with ragworm and peeler crab the prime baits.

Fishing from the very tip of the small **Goathorn peninsula** can be particularly rewarding during autumn night tides for eels and flounders. The South Deep Channel runs very close to the shoreline and offers sport four hours either side of high water. Peeler crab is the killer bait.

Jerrys and **Gravel Points** are the best flounder marks in the harbour as far as the beach angler is concerned. During December and January, 2 lb plus fish are common and there's the possibility of a 3-pounder. A big flood tide and ragworm bait are the winning combination. Distance casting is not needed; a 50-yard lob puts your bait among the fish. Flatties turn up through the summer and autumn months, although crabs and very small bass can make fishing difficult, while the odd plaice can never be ruled out.

The dramatic and beautiful **Isle of Purbeck** coast offers the shore angler some of the finest and most varied fishing anywhere in the British Isles. The breathtaking scenery is often over-shadowed by the sheer scale of sport, including giant conger, big bass, shy mullet and record-breaking wrasse.

The flat and sandy beach at **Studland**, which is backed by sand dunes just west of Poole harbour, is worth fishing for flounders during the winter months. There's also good plaice during the summer and bass when a good surf is running. The last three hours of the flood tide, are, without question, the best fishing times, although occasionally fish are taken over the low-tide period during very big tides. Best baits include lugworm, white rag and razorfish for the flatties, with live sandeels sorting out the better bass.

Sweeping **Swanage Bay** is refuge for many anglers during south-westerly gales, although it's one of those frustrating beaches which seems to switch on and off for no apparent reason. The rocks, on its eastern fringe, provide pollack, wrasse, small conger and the odd bass throughout the summer and winter months. Towards the centre of the bay sole, flounders, pouting, plaice and even the occasional ray can be taken at night, especially during settled weather. Fish the small pier at the western end of the bay during daylight for mullet, wrasse, mackerel and pollack or fish at night for conger.

Fast tides churn up the seabed and release a constant food supply around **Peveril Point**, which guards the western end of Swanage Bay. The ground here is rough with summer species including wrasse along with small pollack, mullet and bass. Best baits are ragworm, peeler crab and sandeels. Lures are also the downfall of many fish. The young flood tides always brings in more fish.

Durlston Bay is a shallow rocky mark holding big wrasse from September to early October. Mullet also appear in numbers when the sea is flat, calm and clear, although they are difficult to catch unless approached with caution. Very small baited spinners do well. At the far western end of the bay, directly under **Durlston Head**, is a superb conger mark. A flat shelf of rock makes an ideal fishing platform, although this mark should only be approached in calm conditions. The slightest swell pushes the sea over the ridge towards the top end of the tide. You will also be cut off two hours either side of high-water springs.

This very deep-water mark is swept by a strong tidal current on the flood, so tackle needs to be robust. The cliff overhang hampers long-distance casting here, but don't worry – it isn't needed. This is a prime conger mark. Drop a fillet of fresh mackerel 30 yards out on a night tide and wait for the fun as eels from between 15 lb and 25 lb home in on the scent trails. Fish between 30 lb and 40 lb are on the cards during October and November. Good-size pollack, the odd double-figure bass, wrasse and smaller pollack provide the action during daylight sessions.

Moving west, **Dancing Ledge** is the next accessible fishing spot, although it's not the easiest place to approach. You have to drive a couple of miles out from Swanage and then there's a hike across several fields before descending down a never-ending cliff path to the sea. I normally fish here in summer armed with a light carp rod and fixed-spool reel filled with 6 lb line in search of big wrasse, pollack and mullet. There's almost 15 feet of water directly under your feet, so you will need a sliding float rig to allow the ragworm bait to dance in the tide off the bottom. A tiny baited spinner worked through the kelp will also attract fish, especially pollack. It's a known conger mark during autumn with fresh mackerel or pollack baits attracting fish.

The old quarries at **Windspit Point** make an ideal fishing platform, especially during rough and stormy conditions. Again, it is not an easy venue to approach and it involves a one and a half mile hike from the small village of Worth Matravers, which can be exhausting during hot, muggy conditions. Rough ground is a tackle graveyard, so fish with 30 lb to 40 lb mainline.

Daylight visits produce wrasse nudging 6 lb, with a record-breaker very much on the cards during November. Good pollack and bass are also taken on ragworm, hermit and peeler crab baits. Conger seem easy to catch from this venue – sometimes it seems difficult not to catch them! Fresh mackerel is easily the top bait, but a large drop net or flying gaff is essential to lift the hooked fish up to where you are fishing. **Seacombe Cliff** lies half a mile west of Windspit and is capable of producing wrasse, conger and pollack. It is a difficult mark to both reach and fish. The small bay at **Chapman's Pool** holds bass, wrasse, pollack, conger and a few flatfish in summer. It is approached by a fair walk from Worth Matravers, but care is needed because of the crumbling cliff. Never venture here alone.

Kimmeridge Bay is a shallow-water mark noted for its bass and mullet taken on light tackle techniques. Catching Kimmeridge mullet can be extremely frustrating because you can often see them feeding on the seaweed fly maggots washed out of the decaying weed. A fly rod comes to the rescue in this situation. Bait a small floating hook with a single maggot collected from the seaweed rafts and cast it to the feeding mullet. Roaming bass can be taken on standard bottom tackle, although many good fish are taken on plugs and lures, particularly during rough sea conditions.

Warbarrow Bay is a magic venue, with its steeply shelving shingle beach dropping away into deep water holding conger, dogfish, wrasse, rays, pollack and flatties. The bay lies in the middle of the Ministry of Defence Lulworth firing ranges and can only be approached by foot from the deserted village of Tyneham. To the left of the bay, **Warbarrow Tout** juts out, creating a strong tide race, where large conger, pollack and even the odd tope have been taken in summer.

There's a small sandbar towards the centre of the bay, where plaice and rays can be taken from early spring onwards, while the far rocky western end of the bay again produces more conger, pollack and a few loner bass. During January there's the chance of latching on to a double-figure pollack if you use squid bait. A flood tide topping out around midnight brings the best rewards.

Mupe is another small east-facing shingle bay sited close to the army ranges. It's not so deep as Warbarrow, but conger still show in good numbers at night throughout the autumn. There's small wrasse during the day on ragworm and crab baits.

The picturesque **Lulworth Cove** provides a sheltered haven during rough and windy conditions. In summer it is extremely busy, with small boats anchored a few yards offshore. Bass, conger, wrasse and pouting can be taken on leger gear in autumn. At the eastern entrance to the cove there's a rocky platform where you can spin or fish with light float tackle for small pollack, wrasse, garfish and mullet.

Durdle Door is a popular holiday beach during the summer months, but quiet autumn nights can bring huss, conger and rays, although the odd specimen sole, plaice and pouting can never be ruled out. Fish a flooding tide with ragworm, fresh mackerel, squid and crab baits for the best results. The beach can only be reached by a very steep cliff path.

Back in the sixties **Ringstead Bay** was a noted conger and

Bull huss, like this finely marked fish, can be caught from the Isle of Purbeck shoreline, especially after dark

plaice mark, but in recent years there's been a decline in sport. Conger are still taken at night from the rocky areas, while the odd plaice does occasionally show, but they are few and far between. Small pollack and wrasse happily still rattle rod-tips.

An area of far-ranging extremities lies between the shallow, sandy beaches of Weymouth Bay to a hostile tidal race that sweeps past **Portland Bill**. Access to some of Portland's rock marks are extremely dangerous and for this reason I have only listed those which are reached relatively easily. However, I want to stress that even these should be approached with great caution.

Redcliff, a fairly steep shelving shingle beach with rocky out-crops, is worth fishing at night. During autumn specimen-size sole feed well on ragworm bait. It's also a noted conger mark with fish of 30 lb a possibility, along with pollack, pouting, plaice and dogfish.

Weymouth's popular **Preston Beach** is a non-starter during the summer holiday season. The beach is better throughout the winter, with lugworm the top bait. Night tides produce flounders, pouting, dabs and small whiting, while the odd bass can be expected during stormy periods.

Busy **Weymouth harbour** provides a safe refuge for mullet during the summer with fish to 4 lb possible on light float tackle. The western side of the harbour produces the better fish; also a noted flounder mark with pouting, pollack and the odd coalfish feeding at night.

Weymouth's **Stone Pier**, to be found on the western side of the harbour entrance, fishes all year and is an extremely popular and safe venue for youngsters. A light float tackle approach in summer brings pollack, wrasse, mackerel, garfish, mullet, scad and whiting. Legered baits sort out flatties, pouting and even the odd codling in autumn.

Situated mid-way along the eastern side of Portland, **Church Ope Cove** offers sport throughout both the summer and autumn months. Wrasse and conger are the main species, although a few good-size pollack, dogfish and plaice are sometimes taken. Hermit crab and ragworm sort out the wrasse during daylight, while a fillet of fresh mackerel is a killer at night for conger. Spinning from the rocks on either side of the bay lures small pollack and the odd bass.

The rock marks of **Cheyne** are approached through the old quarries just east of the small village of Southwell. A sewer pipe runs out into the centre of the small rocky bay, where conger hide up. Wrasse and pollack can be taken by day with a flood tide again a must. An extremely fast tide rip occurs during the ebb tide which makes fishing unrealistic. The water to the right of the pipe is slightly deeper and normally turns up the better fish.

The flat-topped **Pulpit Rock** is the most popular Portland rock mark. The only way to reach the top of the rock is to scramble up the side of a huge slab of rock leaning against the stack, using footholds chiselled out years ago. The platform on top of the rock, which stands some 30 feet above sea level, is relatively small and there's only enough space for three or four anglers. Tides and bait are critical; a strong tidal race sweeps past the end of Portland with the exception of three hours either side of low water, and it's during this period that the better catches are taken.

If you are looking for specimen-size wrasse then fish velvet swimming crabs between October and December. Ragworm and hermit crab will take smaller fish to 4 lb. The venue also produces a variety of other species such as conger, pollack and bass. Good bags of pollack are possible during early spring on float-fished white ragworm.

Situated mid-way along the western side of Portland, near Blacknor Point, **Ocean Rock** is worth fishing three hours either side of low water for conger eels. This is an extremely rough and snaggy mark so tackle needs to be strong. Don't mess about with small baits and hooks as the fish often run big, and once hooked, test the toughest tackle. Autumn sees the best catches, especially during settled weather.

The 18 miles of continuous shingle which forms the famous **Chesil Beach** attracts shore anglers like a magnet. However, anglers should note that access is extremely limited and often a long hike or a short boat trip across the Fleet, which runs behind the bank, is needed to reach the fishing areas. A large area of the bank is also fenced off during the nesting season.

The deep-water **Chesil Cove**, where Chesil Beach merges with the rocks of Portland, offers a safe refuge for many species, including conger and wrasse. These can be taken in numbers during the autumn period with a flood tide a must. Hermit crabs seem to come out on top for the wrasse, while fresh mackerel sort out the bigger eels.

The stretch of Chesil opposite **Ferry Bridge**, which carries the main road to Portland, is noted for the two wrecks which lie just offshore well within casting range. Situated at either end of the car park, they hold pollack, pouting, conger and even the occasional hefty angler fish. Autumn brings fishing to a peak, although a spring run of codling does occasionally occur. For general fishing try ragworm or lugworm, although peeler crab can often pick out the better codling. Mackerel turn up in fair numbers during summer and garfish are often taken on light float tackle during September and October. Fishing off the Ferry Bridge itself with light spinning tackle brings pollack and coalfish, while flounders and some hefty bass run up the **Fleet**.

The area of beach directly in front of the **Bridging Camp** is prime cod ground throughout the winter months. Whiting, dabs and dogfish are also taken. A fair tide runs along this beach during a flooding tide and a 5 oz or 6 oz Breakaway-type lead is a must. When the water is coloured following a storm, drop a big fish bait at short range for conger. The action can be tremendous.

The **Moonfleet** stretch of the bank is only accessible by dinghy, but the fishing can be superb throughout the autumn as hefty cod, conger, dabs and whiting feed. Lugworm, hermit and peeler crab all fish well, particularly when the cod are in. The first two hours of the flood and high water are the peak fishing periods.

Langton Herring is another limited-access venue and again a dinghy is needed to cross the Fleet. As with Moonfleet, fishing can be fantastic with many double-figure cod, including 20-pounders, taken every year. Tides and baits are similar to Moonfleet.

During the summer months vast shoals of mackerel patrol close to the **Abbotsbury** shore line, followed by many larger predatory species. This is one of those rare beaches where any species could turn up, from double-figure smoothhound to 40 lb conger. Other visitors include whiting, pouting, dabs, plaice, drogonettes and dogfish. The area of beach known as the **Dragons Teeth**, just to the east of Abbotsbury, is the favoured cod mark, while dabs and smoothhound turn up towards the western end of the venue. A flood tide certainly produces the better catches, while all the popular baits have their day, although as far as I'm concerned lugworm and peeler crab come out top.

West Bexington offers easy access and parking. Plaice are the main target species during the early part of the year and the first fish normally put in an appearance around early March, peaking in June, when mackerel and dabs are then the dominant species. Best plaice catches normally happen during long settled spells when the sea is flat and clear. Distance casting with lugworm and white rag brings the best bags. As autumn approaches small whiting start to take up residence along with the first of the winter's cod. The odd turbot can also never be ruled out.

Cogdon is a superb spring plaice mark, with anglers often taking up to 20 fish a session, especially towards the eastern end of the venue. Lugworm and white rag fished at distance do the damage, with an hour either side of high water being prime fishing time. Mackerel show in force throughout the summer; whiting in

Chesil Beach, to the west of Portland, is the perfect all-year-round venue. Here we see a near 10 lb cod caught on worm

winter. This is another beach where anything is on the cards, especially during the autumn. Parking and access are easy.

West Bay beach, just to the west of the small coastal town, offers interesting sport during summer and autumn with mackerel, dogfish, flatfish, pouting and pollack. The concrete groynes protecting the small harbour entrance make ideal fishing platforms, where lively garfish, mackerel and scad can be taken on light spinning tackle. The harbour itself is renowned for its large head of mullet.

Seatown's relatively shallow beach is capable of producing bass during stormy periods. Small plaice seem ever present along with dabs, pouting and small whiting. Hope for the odd ray during the summer months.

Rocky outcrops can be found at either end of **Charmouth beach**, where hefty conger, rays and bass can be caught. During autumn large numbers of pouting feed on night flood tides with virtually any bait taking fish. Come winter there's even the chance of a big cod. The stretch of beach known as **Black Cliff**, lying mid-way between Charmouth and Lyme Regis, is a noted autumn conger mark. Fish up to 30 lb have been taken here on fresh mackerel bait. Care should be taken when fishing over big spring tides, as you can easily get cut off.

Lying on Dorset's extreme western border, **Lyme Regis** offers the beach angler a variety of marks to fish. The harbour wall attracts wrasse, conger, mackerel, garfish and pollack throughout the summer and autumn periods, while the small pebbly beach, just west of the harbour, produces decent fish at night. Autumn species include large pouting, dogfish and conger. The sandy beach to the east of the harbour offers small flatfish in daylight and pouting and strap conger at night. The beach does get crowded during the peak holiday period.

Tackling the Dorset boat marks

THERE'S no doubt about it, the Dorset boat angler is spoilt for choice. Every type of mark imaginable is within easy reach, ranging from the quiet inshore waters of Poole harbour to the mad tidal race off Portland Bill. Deep-water wrecks abound — there are over 150 known hulks, all offering a safe haven for monster conger, ling and pollack. Even sharks show in summer months.

Six ports are the home of a large fleet of charter angling boats, offering trips lasting just a few hours over inshore marks to 24-hour wrecking sessions. And for the angler trailing his own dinghy there are plenty of launching sites to get his craft afloat from.

Bait is certainly the key to hauling fish over the gunwale,

especially over the many inshore marks, where the smaller species are to be found feeding. For the deep-water marks, including wreck marks, top bait isn't so critical, although even here the correct bait has a role to play in a successful day's fishing. Mackerel is without question the number one bait throughout the warm summer months with nearly every species readily accepting a nice fresh fillet, cutlet or slice. The first mackerel shoals normally appear towards the end of April, although there can be a slight variation depending on water temperature and weather conditions. The fish stay right through the summer with catches peaking during August. Many are still taken during the autumn period, although by the end of October their numbers rapidly dwindle. On most boat trips the skipper will stop for a few minutes' feathering to fill the bait box.

A double squid bait mounted on a 6/10 hook is a killer for large cod during the winter months, especially in Bournemouth Bay. Supply is no problem – there are many tackle shops throughout the region which sell frozen squid. Fresh squid is available from Portland during autumn.

Fresh sandeels are deadly for bass, especially when fishing over either the Portland or Peveril races. Many other species, such as dogfish, plaice, pollack and turbot, love the taste of sandeel. Frozen eels are again available from most tackle shops along the coast, while fresh sandeels can be bought from Poole quay in season.

Both ragworm and peeler crab are favoured baits among dinghy anglers working in Poole harbour. Peeler crab also accounts for hefty smoothhound and plaice hauls. Mackerel strip tipped with a big juicy lugworm is deadly when drifting for plaice.

Pirks, large artificial metal lures which send out vibrations like a fish, are certainly an essential item of tackle when heading for the many deep-water wrecks, where ling, pollack, coalfish and cod are the main target species. These pirks are often baited. Artificial lures, such as the Red Gill, prove very effective for pollack, particularly when drifting over inshore wrecks and through Portland race, where bass will be taken. The Shambles Bank is another area where Red Gills often come into their own, taking codling, pollack, whiting and the odd coalfish.

Selecting the right tackle to deal with so many varied marks and types of fishing could leave you scratching your head. The days of short, stiff rods and lines that completely out-match the fish are thankfully gone, although in some areas heavier kit is required to cope with both strong tidal rips and heavy weed.

For general boat fishing off Dorset I would personally settle for a 20 lb class boat rod, which is normally more than adequate to cope with most species encountered. There are occasions, however, when a 30 lb or even 50 lb class rod may be needed, particularly when wrecking. The strong tides rushing along the English Channel call for fairly heavy leads and sometimes 2 lb plus sinkers are needed to get a bait down to the fish. To cut down drag, wire line is often used. In such situations it is essential to use a rod fitted with a roller tip, or better still a rod fitted out completely with roller rings. These rods should be chosen with care, as there are some inferior rollers fitted to some rods.

Uptiding, or boatcasting, is also popular, especially in the Bournemouth Bay area, over Christchurch Ledge and near the Shambles Bank: A nine-and-a-half foot rod capable of handling 6 oz leads fits the bill nicely. Always keep the rod as light as possible so you can hold it at all times and not miss bites. See the Hampshire chapters if you want to know more about boatcasting.

A light spinning rod is a necessary tool for catching flatfish in Poole harbour and for drifting near the southern entrance to Portland harbour, where pollack can be taken in numbers.

Shark fishing is very specialised, calling for heavy-duty outfits, although even here anglers are turning their attention to light-line class fishing. Personally, I'm not in favour of scaling tackle down too much, for I hate the thought of a fish swimming around with snapped-off tackle dangling from its jaw.

There are many middleweight reels that team with the 20 lb and 30 lb class rods which cover nearly all the fishing situations to be found off the Dorset coast. Models that I particularly like include those from the Shimano and the ABU 7000 and 9000 series. The only other type of reel you are likely to need is a lightweight fixed-spool reel for harbour fishing.

With such varied boat fishing it would be wise to carry a selection of conventional bell leads ranging from a couple of ounces up to a couple of pounds or more, plus a few spiked Breakaway sinkers for uptide work. Most nylon lines available are suitable. Personally, I would go for either Maxima or Drennan Sealine – 15 lb breaking strain for uptiding and 30 lb for bottom fishing.

Dorset's noted boat angling marks

BOAT fishing along the Dorset coast can be divided into four distinct regions; Mudeford, in the east of the county, to St Aldhelms Head, the dinghy marks within Poole harbour, the ground from St Aldhelms Head to Portland and, finally, Lyme Bay.

West Bay harbour, home to a small fleet of charter fishing boats

Mudeford, situated in the entrance to Christchurch harbour, has a small charter boat fleet with craft heading out to both **Christchurch Ledge** and the **Needles** area. Dinghy anglers are attracted to the area because they can fish in the lee of **Hengistbury Head** during south-westerly blows for plaice, pollack, mackerel, wrasse and conger during the summer, while a few hefty cod are boated during the winter months. Dinghy launching facilities are available, although the area does get very busy during the summer.

Christchurch Ledge stretches out from the shore at Hengistbury Head for a distance of just over three miles. During the warm summer months it attracts bream, plaice, rays, pollack, conger, wrasse and dogfish, while in winter there's hefty cod and whiting.

Poole is the home of the largest charter fleet in the county, with boats offering every conceivable type of boat angling from short summer mackerel trips through to sharking. Several tackle shops along Poole quay act as booking agencies and can supply bait to order. The clean, sandy bottom of **Poole Bay** holds plenty of plaice in summer along with some good-size rays, although many boats head further afield to the rocky grounds off **Peveril Point** in search of conger, bream, pollack, rays and dogfish.

Durley Rocks, situated a quarter of a mile south-west of Bournemouth pier, are normally alive with small fish during summer. They shelter among the rough ground on an otherwise featureless seabed.

The small resort town of **Swanage** boasts several charter boats running angling trips throughout the summer months. Most boats head for the rough ground off the Purbeck coast in search of conger, rays, pollack, bream and dogfish. Swanage also has launching facilities for small craft, but car parking can be difficult during high summer when the town gets packed with holiday-makers.

Ray are the main target species from the **Swanage Bay** inshore marks. There's also good-size plaice, plus strap conger, wrasse and pollack. **Peveril Race** is a prime bass and pollack mark throughout the summer and autumn months. Best fishing is on the drift with freelined sandeels or Red Gills.

A good target area for bream to 4 lb during August and September is **St Aldhelms Head**, where drifting also produces pollack. Conger and dogfish dominate bottom fishing.

The countless channels in **Poole harbour** offer exceptional sport for the dinghy angler. Flounder and plaice are the dominant species, along with eels, mullet and bass. Plaice fishing begins in May, with some of the bigger fish exceeding 6 lb. Flounder fishing can be hectic and the best of sport occurs during winter, especially the last two weeks in December and the first two weeks in January. There are several dinghy launching sites around the harbour, but the slipway at **Baiter Point** is probably the best place to head for. Parking is available.

Wareham Channel is a superb winter flounder mark with fish over 3 lb taking ragworm baits. During the autumn keep your bait on the move to avoid marauding crabs. A baited flounder spool can also be a killer. The area's very big silver eels are worth fishing for, particularly during October.

The lower reaches of the **South Deep** are certainly favoured plaice marks. Ragworm is the top bait, although peeler crab can also be effective, especially if slowly fished on the drift. Flounders provide lively sport throughout the winter months.

Poole harbour **Main Channel** offers a variety of fishing, although anglers should note that anchoring is not allowed as it is the main shipping lane regularly used by cross-Channel ferries.

A 30 lb boat outfit in full cry off the Dorset coast. There are plenty of rusting wrecks along this part of the coast

Target species include plaice, flounders, eels, pouting, bass, whiting and even the occasional ray.

The **Wych Channel** is a noted winter flounder mark well capable of producing fish over 4 lb. For the best results fish ragworm opposite Patchins Point. In summer mullet can be taken from the higher reaches on baited spinners.

The fierce tides sweeping through the relatively narrow **harbour entrance** churn up the seabed and provide rich feeding for bass. Anglers fishing from small dinghies on the drift pick up exceptional bass on freelined sandeels, artificial Red Gills and spinners. Boat anglers drifting this mark should note that this is a very busy shipping channel used by everything from yachts to cross-Channel ferries. Early morning sessions are strongly advised.

Racing hostile tides ripping around Portland have created massive sandbanks and deep drop-offs in **Weymouth Bay** which offer rich feeding grounds for a multitude of fish. The area is also littered with deep-water wrecks, where huge pollack, coalfish, ling and conger are often caught. Conger, wrasse and pollack can be taken from numerous inshore marks around **Portland** along with the ever present pouting and dogfish. Weymouth shelters a large charter fleet which services the whole area. There are also launching facilities, but dinghy anglers should note that the harbour entrance can be difficult to negotiate in strong south-easterly winds.

Portland harbour offers a safe haven for dinghy anglers in south-westerly winds, and fishing is good for plaice, wrasse, pollack, flounders, dabs and pouting during summer, with whiting and the odd codling taking up residence as winter approaches. Anglers should note that there are restrictions on anchoring in certain areas of the harbour.

The wreck of **HMS Hood** lies at the southern entrance to Portland harbour and offers excellent pollack fishing between April and May. Both Red Gills and sandeels will take fish, although white ragworm is the real killer.

Surprisingly the **Lulworth Bank**, lying approximately two miles south of Lulworth Cove, offers very little sport. The deep drop towards the eastern end of the bank does, however, hold some good pollack from time to time.

The **Adamant Bank** is extremely productive, producing large brill, turbot, dabs, rays and plaice throughout summer and autumn. Whiting arrive in large numbers during the winter, plus the odd good cod and coalfish. Lying on the eastern side of Portland, this mark offers a safe refuge during westerly gales, with the best results occurring on a flood tide peaking just before high water. The wreck of the Dutch steamship **Binnendijk**, which went down in 1939, lies just off the bank and is sometimes alive with pollack and the surprise conger.

The **East** and **West Shambles** is a noted turbot mark, with fish up to 30 lb possible, plus good plaice, brill and dabs. Boats on the drift pick up a number of pollack and codling, and coalfish and whiting are likely to show in winter. Unfortunately the bank does get heavily trawled.

Lying south-west of Portland Bill, the **Kidney Bank** can only be fished during settled periods. The bank is noted for its big blonde rays, which seem to feed hard on ebb tides. Thornback and undulate rays are also in residence along with the odd turbot and brill. There are a few whiting and codling in winter.

Inshore boat fishing in Bournemouth Bay includes plenty of plump pouting

Bass are attracted in numbers to the fast rip of **Portland Race** that sweeps past Portland. The water can become extremely turbulent and rough with overfalls often occurring due to the strong tidal currents. Anglers should be vigilant when approaching this stretch of water. For the best results fish a live sandeel on a long trace.

The wreck of the British steamship *Inisinver*, lying in some 42 metres of water south-west of Portland, holds hefty pollack, ling and conger. Boats working on the drift should pick up the better specimens, with anchoring only possible over slack water.

Lyme Bay is littered with a variety of wrecks, which can hold anything from just a few humble pouting to 70 lb plus conger. There are also several interesting reefs lying only a few miles offshore which abound in marine life. Plaice and dabs are taken in numbers by dinghy anglers fishing only a few hundred yards off **Chesil Beach**. During winter the flatfish are replaced by whiting and large cod. A number of charter boats operate from both **West Bay** and **Lyme Regis** with both night and day charters available. Both ports also offer launching facilities for small boats, but car parking is again restricted during the peak holiday periods, especially at Lyme Regis.

High Ground Reef is a shallow-water reef situated less than a mile off Eype Mouth and is therefore very popular with local charter boats. Many small strap conger, pouting and doggies are taken, although it is not a noted area for specimen-size fish. The small **West Pollack Reef** is named after the large shoals of pollack that often take up residence during the summer months. Lying only half a mile off West Bay it is a favoured spot for dinghy fishing.

The large **East Tennants Reef** lies three miles off Seatown and is often alive with fish. The bottom is extremely rugged, making an ideal refuge for conger, pollack and specimen bass. Only moderated tides sweep this area, making fishing possible at all states of the tide. The **West Tennants Reef** offers a variety of species, including bream, dogs, pouting, pollack, bass and conger.

The wreck of the *Baygintano*, lying only one and a half miles south of Lyme Regis, is one of the most fished wrecks along the South Coast because it holds a multitude of fish such as conger, pollack, pouting, angler fish and dogfish, while rays and plaice can be taken from sandy areas close by. Ideal for the dinghy angler, but don't expect to break any records.

Empress of India is a 14,000-ton battleship lying some 14 miles south-west of Lyme Regis. Its huge hulk is the home of conger along with some very large cod, ling and coalfish. Tides

Offshore expect pollack, like this 16-pounder, cod, ling, conger and coalfish

can be fairly strong, particularly on the flood. The ***Pomerainian*** is another large wreck, lying some seven miles south of Abbotsbury, and is worth visiting for its conger, pollack and cod fishing. Shoals of large pouting congregate around this wreck.

One mile south of **Abbotsbury beach** lies a large reef of the same name. It is very popular with local fishermen, who launch their boats from neighbouring Chesil Beach. In summer expect bream, pollack, pouting, conger, dogfish and flatfish, with whiting and cod taking up residence come winter.

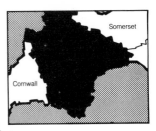

Mike Millman

DEVON

COME to glorious Devon if you want to catch a big fish, says Plymouth's Mike Millman, angler, photographer and journalist. A regular contributor to *Sea Angler* magazine, he tells you how to make the most of the angling opportunities – whether you be local angler or visitor.

AN INTRODUCTION

THE county of Devon has a rugged Channel coastline of some 173 miles occasionally broken by tidal rivers and sweeping bays. Its geography is ever-changing and from the border with Dorset the cliffs are predominantly of yellow clay, which gives way to brilliant white chalk.

From Sidmouth to Torbay blood red sandstone is the warm backcloth to the sea, with grey limestone and granite cliffs standing sentinel to the sea to the border with Cornwall, which is marked by the River Tamar at the great sea port of Plymouth, the South-West's biggest city, which has a population close to 300,000.

At the county's eastern end there are many beaches of sand, shingle and pebbles, all with easy access. The tidal river of the Exe cuts deep inland and the open coast resumes at Dawlish Warren, which is a sand spit rather like New England's Cape Cod, although rather smaller. Its dunes are under constant threat from the sea, but a reclamation programme has established several acres of marram grass and the Warren is now increasing in area, and an important habitat for sea birds.

The River Teign ends its winding journey from the heights of Dartmoor to the sea at Teignmouth. The town has a thriving commercial dock and coasters are constantly coming and going through the narrow tide race between the town beach and Shaldon. The towering mass of the Ness on the Shaldon bank is typical of the high cliffs and rugged nature of the coast round to the major holiday town of Torquay. Steep paths and lanes allow access to several beaches walled in by high ground, but much of this stretch is virtually inaccessible.

A legacy of 19th-century coastal quarrying are the large platforms of rock washed by deep water, which are now popular shore fishing marks. The towns of Torquay, Paignton and Brixham dominate a coast which is largely unspoilt. The population increases dramatically in the holiday season, which is from May to September. Caravan and camping sites and chalet parks exist in vast numbers and almost everywhere you look there is somebody carrying a fishing rod. In good weather places like Hopes Nose are crowded with anglers fishing for flying mackerel and garfish.

The South Hams, south of Dartmouth, is a very picturesque area. There are long beaches of sand and shingle, coves with pine-strewn cliffs and superb estuaries and tidal rivers, where only the calls of the curlew and other wading birds break the silence.

Fishing is a pure joy and there's a good chance you won't see another soul!

Further west are the sand estuaries of the Avon and Erme rivers. Burgh Island in Bigbury Bay, which is separated from the mainland by a tidal causeway, boasts the celebrated 12th-century Pilchard Inn, a noted smugglers' haunt, while the whole area offers excellent shore and dinghy fishing. Big bass are taken on the beach at first light and there are always hungry wrasse to be found in deep kelp-filled gullies.

The south-facing side of Burgh is almost a sheer cliff and the fishing is generally inaccessible. However, an obliging boatman, who can often be found in the Pilchard Inn, can be booked for fishing trips. When the tide washes over the causeway a unique sea tractor makes regular journeys to and from the island in up to ten feet of water.

The final stretch of coast to Plymouth Sound is principally high cliffs with accessible beaches. The Yealm estuary and its tidal river is a haven for those who like messing about in boats. Self-drive craft can be hired at the slipway in front of the Yealm Hotel. Beaches at Heybook Bay and Bovisand are within a few miles of Plymouth. On the other side of the Sound is Cornwall.

Devon enjoys a good climate. During spring and summer the mean average daily duration of sunshine is about six hours. Winters are seldom severe and snow, although often heavy on the high moors, rarely lasts more than a few days on the coast. There is usually a good deal of sun in the depths of winter and crisp bright days are enjoyed in December and January.

In spring and summer the prevailing wind is from the west and south-west. August is usually windy and a percentage of long-range charter trips have to be cancelled. Winds from an easterly direction tend to be very 'fresh' and the old saying 'when the wind is in the east the fish bite least' is unfortunately all too true.

Tidal ranges at the extreme western end of the English Channel are not great and seldom go above five metres during the spring periods. The time from low to high water is close to six and a quarter hours. The strongest flows are in the Start Point area, Lannacombe Bay and over the Skerries Banks. Fishing on the drift is the only way to keep terminal gear on the bottom, where the fish are.

At least 65 different species have been caught by anglers fishing Devon waters and many British records have come from the area. Well in excess of 100 clubs, some with huge memberships, cater for both boat- and shore-fishing enthusiasts. Many belong to the South West Federation of Sea Anglers, which has an eastern boundary between Bristol and Weymouth and embraces the Channel Islands. The Wyvern Division of the National Federation of Sea Anglers is active in Devon and parts of Somerset and Dorset.

Plymouth and Torbay have Federations which serve local interests. Licensed angling clubs are established at Sidmouth, Paignton, Brixham and Dartmouth, while at Plymouth there is a privately owned Sea Angling Centre. It has a fine charter boat marina with a fleet of about 20 craft, many operating throughout the year. Enquire at local tackle shops for more information.

Shore fishing guide to Devon's glorious south coast

THE long and indented Channel coastline of South Devon has dozens of marks worthy of inclusion in a shore fishing guide. The variety of fish they can produce is remarkable and you have only to glance through the British record list for confirmation. Beaches backed by high cliffs are a feature of East Devon, where this chapter begins ...

Axmouth, where fishing is best at the river-mouth after dark on a rising tide. There are several good platforms and a shingle beach from which to cast leger tackle. Peeler crab, marine worms or a cocktail of both is recommended.

Seaton Bridge provides an easy place to fish for bass, but it's only worth a visit after dark. Much the same applies to the beach itself. Bottom gear will take pouting and flatties and there is a good potential for conger.

Beer Beach has rough ground on both its flanks and fishes quite well in the dark hours during a flood tide.

Branscombe, which boasts the longest village street in England, has much to offer even during daylight. The long and steeply shelving beach is rated for bass and in the rocky area wrasse to 4 lb are a popular quarry. During competitions along the East Devon coast Branscombe fish are usually in contention for the prizes. Going westward between the beach and Sidmouth are bass marks supreme, but they are the exclusive territory of men with climbing ability to match mountain goats. As many as six double-figure fish have been taken in a night session and the catch return each year of 6–8-pounders is impressive. Walking the beach to these isolated coves is not recommended as once the tide floods the only way out is up.

Sidmouth still clings to its air of Victorian respectability, although time and development are now having their effect. The species to be expected are bass, flounders, plaice and dogfish. The **Jacobs Ladder** area is rocky and the gullies are hunted by bass after dark. Locals prefer to fish the flood tide when a big surf is running, and on this part of the coast there is plenty of white water. Wrasse of reasonable size are also taken. Leger or paternoster gear baited with peeler crab, marine worms, squid and cuttlefish are successful.

Budleigh Salterton Beach is of shingle and can yield pouting, dogfish and several varieties of flatfish. Bass are also occasionally taken. Mackerel are plentiful in the warm months and provide excellent sport, particularly in the morning and late evening. Sliding float and spinning are the best methods.

Littleham Cove and **Straight Point** offer reasonable sport with wrasse, but fish over 4 lb are a rarity. Pollack, pouting and conger are possible and the area is at its best from half-tide up.

Sandy Bay is a principal holiday resort with many caravan and camping sites. Early morning and late evening fishing is essential if you want to miss the crowds. Long casts with leger gear carrying peeler or soft crab could find a bass, flounder or a plump plaice. Conger to 20 lb are also occasionally taken.

Clock Tower Beach is close to Exmouth and fishes quite well on a rising tide for plaice, dabs, flounder and sometimes bass. Marine worms work, but peeler or soft crab is the best bait to leger.

Exmouth Pier hosts the local sea angling club's headquarters and is a fair mark. In autumn and winter flounder fishing is at its best. With spring come plaice, dabs and bass. The last two hours of the flood tide and the first hour of the ebb are the most productive.

The expansive **River Exe** is principally a small-boat fishing area and a very good one at that. In late autumn and throughout the winter flounder fishing is outstanding with specimens in the 4 lb class often featuring in bags of as many as 40 fish taken in only a few hours. Shore fishing for flounder can be good in the **Starcross** area, but is much better from the Exe-facing side of **Dawlish Warren**. This rather unique sand spit is an excellent fishing area for plaice, dabs and flounder. At the eastern end, which forms a flank at the entrance to the Exe, an 80-yard cast will put a bait − preferably peeler or soft crab − in the deep-water channel. From the south-facing side of the beach a longer cast is required as the water is shallower. Leger and paternoster gear, weighted with grip leads to combat the swift tide run during spring periods, is used. During the winter fat flounder provide

The famous flatfish beaches of Beesands and Hallsands

excellent sport from the north-facing side.

Sea Wall Beach, between Dawlish and Teignmouth, is broken by groynes and rocky outcrops of red sandstone, some carved into fantastic shapes by wind and water. Fishing for bass, plaice, dabs and flounder is fair at times after dark on a flood tide. The ability to cast over 100 yards is an advantage.

The tidal **River Teign** is the best flounder river in Britain. Between late October and the end of February hundreds of fish weighing over 2 lb are taken on peeler and soft-back crab below **Coombe Cellars**. Above the pub, which is right on the beach, all varieties of marine worm will catch. This is on the Shaldon side of the river, where there are a number of paths leading down to small beaches. The British record flounder weighing 5 lb 3 oz 10 drms was taken on a December day by Malcolm Burgess, who was fishing directly in front of the caravan site, half a mile upstream of the bridge.

The **Gasworks** mark on the Teignmouth side can now only be reached by walking along the beach. Behind it the boatyard land is private and the gate which was formerly the access for anglers can only be used by key-holding boat owners. It is an offence to jump the wall and cross the main railway line. Gasworks is rated one of the best flounder marks along the river and has also produced fish of record weight. A couple of miles upstream is the equally productive **Flow Point**. Parking space is extremely limited and it is best to leave vehicles in convenient spots on the main road, which is about 300 yards away from the mark.

At **Teignmouth** the narrow entrance to the river is a popular spot for bass with shore and small-boat anglers. The tide hurtles through the neck and grip leads up to 8 oz are essential if you're fishing from the beach. The boat angler drifts with the tide using live sandeel on a long trace rig. Teignmouth has a commercial fishery for sandeels, which can be purchased at huts on the town beach. Both sides of the river have extensive rows of peeler crab-pots, in reality pieces of guttering and old pipes driven deep into the mud. The 'farms' are privately owned and must not be used as a source of bait.

On the Channel-facing side of the **Ness Headland** there is good bass fishing at night. Local anglers have had specimens weighing over 10 lb here. Most of the fish are taken on live sandeel with peeler crab running a close second. The coastline from the Teign to Torquay is rugged and very productive. There are nearly 20 sea angling clubs in this area of South Devon and the number of fish of specimen weight recorded each year speaks volumes for the quality of the fishing and skill of the anglers.

Petit Tor is a float-fishing area for pollack, mullet, mackerel and garfish. Bottom fishing will produce big wrasse and bass hunt the area after dark, when the tide is flooding. Spinning at first light with a small live sandeel is also a rated time and method for bass and will also take a good bag of mackerel. This stretch of the Torbay coastline has many disused quarries edged by the sea which make superb marks for the shore angler to fish from.

Long Quarry is typical, but the waterline is not easily access-ible. Legering with squid, cuttlefish, mackerel, peeler or soft crab will attract a variety of species. Float fishing is also popular for mullet and mackerel. Conger become active once darkness sets in. **Hopes Nose** is a favourite place for local and visiting anglers. It lies far below Torquay's Marine Drive, but the path, although steep in places, is not difficult. This is big fish country, where wrasse in a class that could break the British record are holed up in underwater caves.

A ballan reliably estimated to weigh at least 12 lb was lost on the surface because the captor wanted to net the specimen himself. The delay in getting a net under it was just what the giant needed and a powerful dive broke the line.

Mackerel and garfish are thick around the Nose in summer.

During school holidays finding a space to cast can be difficult. Plaice and dabs are frequently landed by club anglers and there is also good mullet fishing. On the right-hand flank of the outcrop, some 300 yards away from the most popular parts, is a sewer outfall. If you can stand the atmosphere large mullet could be yours, as there are many in the turgid water.

Fishing is with a sliding float rig baited with bread or mackerel flake. In the sewer area groundbaiting is unnecessary, but it is vital elsewhere. A mix of bread and minced fish is placed in an onion sack and hung so that it is partly submerged. The movement of the water constantly releases particles, which soon draw the fish in. Mackerel and pollack are also attracted and can be a nuisance if your mind is set on mullet.

From the Nose to Torquay harbour the coastline is very rugged above and below deep water. Its claim to angling fame is conger. Giants, including the British record shore-caught fish of 67 lb 1 oz, often come fighting to the surface. In no way is the quality of fishing declining, as recent captures include a specimen of 62 lb 6 oz and many topping 40 lb have been hauled ashore. Equipment must include a couple of powerful pressure lamps and several gaffs with heads securely fastened to stout poles. Gaffs with screw-in hooks are useless against a fish that can spin like a top. Heavy-duty tackle is essential for this tough but very exciting specialist type of shore fishing.

Beaches, and there are many between Torquay and Brixham, are fished by locals, but only after dark when holiday visitors have departed. During the winter there is a great deal of fishing activity in the early morning and late evening and during the night, when the main target is bass. Excellent catches are made with the frozen peeler crab. Plaice and dabs also feature in autumn and winter fishing.

Haldon and **Princess Piers** offer easy fishing for mackerel, garfish, pollack and several other species in summer. In the cold months good whiting are taken, along with flounder and dab.

At **Brixham** there is much for the shore enthusiasts, although restrictions are being brought about by new development and a growing level of commercial and holiday craft movement. There is a possibility that sections of the long breakwater could be restricted on the harbour-facing side, particularly in the vicinity of the oil refuelling jetty. The breakwater has always been a good fishing area. Large conger are frequently caught after dark. Mackerel, pollack, garfish and mullet are common throughout the summer and autumn months. The best mullet fishing is from the inside edge. Small-boat anglers do well fishing in the vicinity

One of the fat River Teign flounders

of the commercial fish docks and market. The rocky ground at **Shoalstone** on the west side of the breakwater gives bass, pollack and mackerel. Float gear carrying live sandeel, peeler crab or marine worms should be tried two hours before and two hours after high water. Spinning for mackerel is good just as dawn breaks. It is also prime time for bass.

Berry Head Quarry, now disused, gives the best shore fishing in Torbay. Deep water holding most of the popular species is at your feet and there is something to catch 12 months of the year. Float fishing is excellent for mullet, mackerel, pollack, garfish and coalfish. Legering produces wrasse, bull huss, cod and a variety of flatfish. There is also a fair chance of taking a bass or two on live sandeel. The British record mackerel was caught here, a monster of 5 lb 11 oz 14 drms, which fell to float gear.

Cars must be left in the public car park on the edge of the Berry Head Country Park. Disabled anglers are permitted to drive their cars down to the water's edge, but a key for the gate must be obtained from the Countryside Ranger, who has an office on the headland. He is available between 9 a.m. and 5 p.m..

Anglers who wish to fish at night must also obtain a key, which is numbered and recorded, between the stated times. The key must be posted in the office letter-box on leaving. Creaming water around the great mass of Berry Head hides hunting bass and it's also a first-rate area for ballan wrasse, with fish up to 10 lb a possibility. In winter double-figure pollack come within casting range and there is good sport with cod. Bottom fishing is the principal method for these species. A sliding float rig is used for mullet, mackerel and garfish. Live sandeel is a favourite bait for the headland marks. Access to the water is very difficult and **no attempt** should be made to go down without a local expert as a guide.

Dartmouth is a popular holiday town and within a few miles there is a wide choice of shore and boat fishing. It's the principal port for trips to the fabulous Skerries Banks, which is covered in the accompanying boat section.

There is good fishing from rocks on both sides of the estuary for plaice, dabs and ray. There are also plenty of wrasse in the deep clefts at the base of cliffs on the east flank, which can be reached by well-defined paths and a final clamber to suitable platforms.

Bass penetrate far into the tidal river and the **Anchor Stone** area just below Greenway Quay is a fine mark during a flooding spring tide. Dinghy anglers driftlining live sandeel do very well and also take good thornback ray from the depressions in the river bed a mile downstream, just as the Naval College comes into view.

On summer evenings, when the tide is high, there is lively sport with mackerel on float gear from the town's harbour wall, which runs for over half a mile between the higher and lower ferries. Mullet are numerous in the Dart, especially in the harbour area and upstream of Dittisham. Greenway Quay, which is opposite, is reached by road from Galmpton. The rocky ground at **Scabbacombe**, which is an open coast mark, offers fine wrasse fishing and is also good for bull huss, cod and conger.

Blackstone Point is an excellent rock mark for all the usual species. Float fishing is popular owing to the snaggy nature of the ground, but for big wrasse a leger rig should be used. Peeler and soft crab are the best baits for the bottom and it's live prawn or sandeel with the float tackle.

Slapton Beach stretches for several miles and has steeply shelving shingle. The configuration is constantly changing due to the strong surf, which is a feature of the area. A cast of 50 yards will put a leger bait in 20 feet of water and doubling the distance finds a long ridge of sand behind which plaice and dabs congregate, particularly along the stretch directly in front and to the sides of the memorial, which is approximately half-way along the beach. Slapton is the principal venue in the South-West for shore competitions, and is capable of accommodating over 200 anglers. It's popular year-round and although used extensively by holidaymakers in the summer it is always possible to find plenty of room for long-distance casting. During the winter plaice, dabs, coalfish and cod are the usual species. The main run of plaice begins in the spring and soon after there is steady sport with mackerel and garfish. Flounder and small turbot are also caught. Reasonable fishing is to be had by day, but the best action comes at dusk and during darkness.

Two miles beyond Torcross the road swings to **Beesands** and **Hallsands**, a pair of fishing villages steeped in history which offer the same species as Slapton. The former is the busier, having a large holiday caravan park on the eastern side. It boasts the Cricket Inn, which is almost on the beach. In winter it's often the case that more anglers are inside at the bar than on the shingle, and in summer when the holidaymakers are about you have to fight your way to the bar.

Start Point is reached by a narrow road with passing places to a fair-size car park. It's a stiff walk and climb down to the rocks on either side of the headland. The point is dominated by a lighthouse and is out of bounds. The trek can be well worthwhile as float-fished crab or live prawn can be quickly snapped up by a sizeable bass. There are good wrasse in the gullies and mullet haunt the headland coves. On the east side, the bottom is less rocky and the cove is visited by several varieties of ray, which take live sandeel legered on single-hook rigs.

Although now few in number, black bream come to the area in autumn. Some years ago, I recall taking seven to 3½ lb in an afternoon, but such days are unlikely to return.

There is useful ground to the west of the Start, which can be reached from the coastal path. The first break in the cliffs is at **Lannacombe**, which is accessible by road. Turbot, plaice, dabs and several other species are on the catch list during a spring flood tide. The rocky ground is good for bass, pollack and mackerel; here live prawn works well on a float rig, with the band set to maintain the bait just above the kelp.

Prawle Point is much visited by wrasse hunters, who beat 5 lb quite easily in the summer and autumn. Mullet are in the coves and inlets at this time of the year and a stealthy approach, plenty of groundbaiting and very light float gear should produce good action. Sandy patches in the coves definitely hold good ray, but the area is seldom fished after dark. If it were there could be a few surprises.

Salcombe is a top area for the angler, and its shore and boat fishing is of outstanding quality. Rocks on both sides of the huge estuary are very popular and with good reason. Most of the flatfish types are at one time or another on the flat sandy bottom and, further upstream, the long stretch of beach at Portlemouth is also an excellent mark. Plaice to 7½ lb, dabs in the 2 lb class and flounder touching 3½ lb usually head a year's best fish list. At **The Castle**, which is close to South Sands on the west side of the river, wrasse to 8 lb can be expected from the shore, while the small-boat angler fishing around the marker poles can expect superior sport.

Starehole Bay is edged by accessible rocks and the sandy ground attracts good numbers of flatfish. More difficult to reach are the rocks under the towering mass of **Bolt Head**, although the effort can be more than worthwhile as the nightmare terrain holds huge wrasse. Dinghy anglers have had many fish in the 6 to 8½ lb class, but the weather must be very settled to fish the mark. The gilt head bream, which is rare everywhere else in the South-West, is a regular visitor to Salcombe. It arrives in late April and stays until the autumn. British records have been set in both the shore and boat categories and the potential, now that more anglers are aware of their presence, is limitless. In the vicinity of the estuary sandbar, which can be dangerous for small-

Brixham's long breakwater makes an ideal fishing platform

boat anglers in rough weather, there are fine bass to be had on live sandeel. Flounder make their way upstream from Salcombe in the early autumn and fishing is excellent right through the winter in the Kingsbridge estuary and the creeks, which cut deep into the countryside.

South Pool and **Frogmore** are extremely popular venues. The average weight of flounder is a high 2 lb, with many scaling close to 3 lb. Legered peeler crab followed by marine worm are the preferred baits.

The beaches of **Thurlestone, Bantham** and **Bigbury**, are rated bass territory. From April there is the chance of double-figure fish at dawn and dusk during a flooding spring tide. At Bantham begin fishing at the mouth of the river and work back with the flooding tide as far as the narrow neck. The neck, which is a very good spot to ambush fish as they head upriver, can be reached through the sand dunes, which are close to a large car park. Razor fish, live sandeel — which in the summer can be dug and raked from the sand at the water's edge — peeler and soft crab are the best baits for leger fishing. Good flounder can be caught from the shoreline in the Avon and Erme rivers to the limit of the saltwater run. The fishing is very good from autumn to early spring. A variety of rays can be found on the beaches in this area.

Stoke Point is the best mark along Devon's long coast for small-eyed ray, with specimens being taken in late summer and autumn. This species is only active after dark and sandeel, preferably live, seems to be the exclusive bait. Frozen sandeel is also much used and reasonably successful. There are plenty of suitable ledges on the west side which are reached from the coastal path. Baits should be dropped on to clean sand between the rocky outcrops. Visit the area during low tide conditions so that the ground configuration can be studied. This will pay a handsome dividend during night sessions. Specimen-sized spotted ray are also found in this area and there is a possibility of blondes. Stoke is also good for pollack; fish to 14 lb have been taken and the best bass from the ground weighed in at 14¾ lb. Big, tough wrasse hide out in the mass of gullies which stretch all the way to the mouth of the River Yealm. Some of the clefts under the disused lookout station hold 30 feet of water at low tide and this is where the wrasse hide in the crannies covered by a thick veil of weed.

The nearby **Hilsea** and **Blackstone Points** are very good wrasse marks, as is **Gara Point** and the rocks around to **Mouthstone**. From here the productive ray grounds can be reached and there is always the possibility of a bass. In the tidal river the winter flounder marks at **Cofflete creek** and **Puslinch Bridge**, which is as far as the saltwater goes, produce hundreds of large fish to 4 lb. These marks are far from the open sea and at least one hour above the time printed on tide tables for low water must be allowed for the water to arrive.

On the west side of the estuary is **Season Point**, a top mark after dark for small-eyed ray, thornback and spotted ray. Good bass are also taken here at times. **Renney Rocks** at Heybrook

Bay is excellent for grey mullet and it's one of the few places where they are caught on bottom gear. The usual light float tackle rig does, however, take the majority of fish. Groundbaiting soon brings them within range. There are many deep gullies with a covering of kelp holding big wrasse. Plot the clear sandy strips between the rocks at low tide and leger crab or king ragworm. The high front rocks are cut off by the tide around mid-water and it is essential to keep a watchful eye if you don't want to be marooned.

Plymouth Breakwater, constructed from four million tons of stone, is home for a wide variety of fish and provided you are armed with a long-handled net the fish can be landed without difficulty. However, first you need to book a boat ride in advance from one of the craft that regularly take visitors and anglers out to the fascinating structure. Wrasse abound in the thick kelp weed and fish to 6 lb are taken on leger gear, although the terrain is hard on end tackle. Grab is the best bait, but king ragworm is a good second. Fair pollack fishing can be had if you cast light float tackle baited with worm. The big fish come from the ends of the breakwater, and the trick is to let the tackle drift well away with the tide before starting a steady retrieve.

Thornback are common, but the best catches are made near the east end and close to the old fort at the centre. Peeler crab is the most successful bait and should be offered on a single-hook leger. Allow plenty of time for the ray to swallow the bait after you feel the first bite. Grey mullet provide plenty of sport, but you must remember that very light groundbaiting is essential.

Plymouth has long been one of the premier sea angling centres in the country and boasts over 40 sea angling clubs. **Western Kings**, at the entrance to the River Tamar, is regarded as the best shore conger mark in the South-West. Fish to 45 lb have been dragged on to the concrete hardstanding, which is fronted by more than 100 feet of water at half-tide. A mile upstream is the small stone pier of **Mutton Cove**, which is also a much rated mark for large eels. Fishing must be after dark and the best bait is legered squid or cuttlefish.

Rusty Anchor, **West Hoe Pier**, **Elphinstone** and the rocks under **Plymouth Hoe** are also worth a visit. The rocks under the Hoe's Lion's Den have produced conger to 54½ lb and many a good bass.

DEVON'S BAIT BEDS

Seaton River:	Lugworm, ragworm.
Chiselbury Bay:	Lugworm, ragworm, prawns.
Exe Estuary:	Lugworm, ragworm.
River Teign:	Lugworm, ragworm, crab (soft-back and peeler) — don't touch the line of pots), mussels and sandeels below the bridge.
Torbay area:	Lugworm, ragworm (can be dug from many beaches at low tide), razorfish, mussels. Net for prawns in the harbours.
Brixham Breakwater:	Prawns, mussels, limpets.
Brixham Breakwater-Shoalstone:	Prawns, limpets.
River Dart, Upper reaches:	Crab (soft-back and peeler), ragworm, lugworm.
Salcombe Estuary:	Ragworm, lugworm, prawns in the harbour area and coves; soft-back and peeler crab in the weedy areas.
Bantham, River Avon, Bigbury, River Erme:	Sandeel, ragworm, lugworm, prawns in the coves.
Stoke Point:	Crabs in the rocky area; sandeels on the beach.
River Yealm:	Ragworm, lugworm, prawns; crabs, but they're hard to find.
Plymouth:	Best areas are the Cornish side of the Tamar.
Jupiter Point, Ballast Pond, Forder:	King ragworm, ragworm, lugworm, soft-back and peeler crab.
Lynher Estuary, Forder, Antony Passage:	Ragworm, lugworm, soft-back and peeler crab.
Barbican area:	Prawns.

A hard-fighting thornback ray hits back off Cremyl on the River Tamar

Boat fishing guide to Devon's fish-rich seas

TWO world wars, storms and countless collisions have sent hundreds of vessels to the seabed along the Devon coast, providing a ready-made home for millions of fish. The hulks range in size from trawlers to coasters and from liners to ships of war, and there is now a thriving charter boat industry which takes anglers to sea to sample the spectacular fishing around these marks.

Although there are exceptions, the majority of very big conger, ling, pollack, coalfish and cod captured on rod and line come from wrecks and virtually all the British records have their origins from around the multitude of wrecks.

When wreck fishing began in the late 1950s skippers rarely steamed more than 20 miles from port, so great was the volume of fish inshore. Today it is a very different situation and the average charter could be to a mark lying between 30 and 50 miles from the land. Some craft can even be found in the separation zone of the English Channel, which is almost 60 miles from some western ports.

Extended charters of three to five days give anglers the chance to sample the big fish delights of wrecks lying in the deeper parts of the Channel, and linked with a couple of nights in Guernsey in the Channel Islands, these trips have become extremely popular. Long-range wrecking, however, is totally dependent on 'reasonable' weather conditions. The interpretation of what is reasonable varies from skipper to skipper, and some consider going deep in a Force 5 wind 'quite normal'.

The length of time a charter will last must be considered before you step aboard. Most craft clear port by 7 a.m. and will not return until late in the evening. 12 hours on a wet, heaving deck with the wind tearing at your clothing and sea sickness a fact or threatening can be sheer hell. It is common sense to be fully aware of what you are letting yourself in for and should the weather be definitely dodgy on the day, ask yourself the question, 'Am I up to what may be in store?' and answer it truthfully. If the answer is no or you are even doubtful, pay the skipper his due and head for the nearest café serving breakfast. There is always another and better day!

Skippers only abandon a trip and return to port in a real emergency situation. I am deliberately painting a black picture because far too many would-be wreck anglers go to sea totally

This fine double-figure was caught from the Eddystone Reef off the Devon/ Cornish coast

oblivious of the problems, usually totally ill-equipped, and find conditions far out at sea very different from those inshore. It makes sense to try a few charter trips that leave port at a reasonable hour and have a guaranteed return time before setting out on a deep-water adventure.

True wreck fishing is not a hit-and-miss affair, and a day afloat doesn't come cheap. The average charter fee is about £20, but this can rise to £40, depending on the boat, distance travelled and the reputation of its skipper. Most top-line skippers prefer to charter the whole boat to a group or club.

On occasions a charter party which has found itself short of anglers will allow a freelance angler looking for a berth to come aboard, but first find out what the cost is going to be before agreeing to go afloat. Otherwise you may have a real shock when settling up on returning to port.

The high fees for long-range wrecking reflect the quality of the craft, fuel costs, and the vast amount of sophisticated electronic navigation equipment needed to locate a wreck, colour- and graph-type sounders, radar for safety in poor visibility, a variety of radio aids and the life-saving equipment carried aboard. In exchange for the cash you also get the skipper's considerable expertise.

There are many wreck-fishing ports on the Devon coast. **Plymouth**, which is the major centre in the South-West, has at least 30 licensed craft and some of the best-known skippers in the business. **Salcombe**, **Dartmouth** and **Brixham** have fewer boats collectively, but they are still all top flight. These ports are approximately one hour closer to the great profusion of wrecks lying in the bays of **Start** and **Lyme**, which are much visited by the Plymouth boats.

Wrecks usually hold many conger and even a small hulk can be home to an amazing number of fish. 90-pounders have been hooked at marks standing no more than a few feet off the bottom. Distance is of little consequence with this tough species and just as many, and in some cases more, large fish are taken from marks lying within a dozen miles from land. However, these marks are usually ignored because they have been stripped of pollack and ling, which are the backbone of this type of fishing.

Surprisingly, not all wrecks attract all species. Some are renowned for cod, others produce loads of ling, and there are many noted coalfish and pollack hulks. Leading skippers have all this information to hand in their log books, which contain the vital Decca co-ordinate numbers which enable them to pinpoint exact marks in a seemingly barren waste.

The waters off Devon and Dorset saw much sea and air action in the last war and a vast number of marks are available. Much farther out is the great gash in the seabed called the **Hurd Deep**. Nowhere in the English Channel is the water deeper. 60 fathoms is average and at the north-east end the bottom is 600 feet down.

The best-known wreck in the Hurd is that of the ill-fated submarine *Affray*, which failed to surface after diving off Devon's Start Point in 1951. She lies with her hatches closed and is the grave of 75 men. Anglers have had massive fish from the area and so have commercial fishermen, who regularly take specimens weighing far more than the British rod and line records. A classic example is a pollack of 55 lb, coalfish of 50 lb, cod topping 60 lb and conger as big as 120 lb! Such fish are what dreams are made of.

Deep-water wrecks are usually swept by strong tides, and even during neap periods it is sometimes too strong for anchored-up fishing. This factor alone keeps giant conger reasonably safe. There is a great deal of skill in wreck fishing. If the wind is

Caught aboard a Brixham charter boat, this huge conger eel scaled
104½ lb

against or across the run of tide, accurate positioning of the boat, so that baits end up on or very close to a wreck, is difficult to achieve. It can be very disappointing to encounter an unsuitable wind and tide pattern.

Many wrecks have yet to be discovered in Devon waters, and in the hope of stumbling across one, skippers often keep echo-sounders recording while running to known marks. A thin cone of black, perhaps with a smudge indicating fish above it, could pay dividends provided the skipper can keep the location to himself.

There is good fishing close inshore all along the Devon coastline. Bass are pursued with success near the great sandbar, which lies just off the entrance to **Teignmouth** harbour. And the narrow entrance to the harbour, between **Shaldon** and the town breakwater, is also a favourite spot with local small-boat owners.

The seabed close to the shore between Teignmouth and **Hopes Nose**, which is under very high cliffs, can be extremely productive and is much visited by inshore craft. Bass, conger and wrasse are much sought after and so are plaice, dabs and cod, which are found a little farther out on clean sand.

Just over a mile offshore are several rocky islands in fairly deep water. The **Orestone** is excellent ground for bass, cod and flatties. In the autumn massive mackerel are about. These are predators in every sense and fiercely attack legered baits cut from one of their own kind, squid strip, peeler crab or hermits. Fish weighing nearly 4½ lb provide a high level of sport every year, while samples in the 2 lb class are quite common and pound for pound fight just as hard as any bass on the right tackle.

Thatcher Rock is much closer to the land and a top mark for bass in the early morning, especially during spring, when live sandeel outfishes everything else. This is also a good area for dabs, particularly in winter. Mussel or cockle bait is favourite and often takes up to 100 fish over a tide. The gap between Thatcher Rock and the shore is called the **Gut**, a fine bass mark. Driftlining with live sandeel or live prawn is recommended here.

Within an hour of **Dartmouth** and **Salcombe**, and just three miles out from the South Hams coastline, are the **Skerries**, a series of tide-swept banks of pulverised shell and sand. Although there are fish about all year round, charter boat fishing generally begins in March, when plaice, keen to feed hard after spawning far out at sea, start to arrive. By the end of April craft return with up to 100 fish aboard, caught either on the drift or at anchor. Plaice to 8 lb come from the banks and the yield of fish in the 3 to 4½ lb range is high.

In late April blonde ray arrive and provide excellent fishing for

A Plymouth charter boat leaves the Sea Angling Centre marina

about two months. After this initial burst of activity there is a quieter period until a second wave of plaice hits the Skerries in June.

The turbot season starts around the same time and continues until very late in the autumn. The banks have always been noted for these very large flatfish, which are much prized. A fine specimen flapping on the surface never fails to raise admiring glances.

Sandeel are plentiful on the Skerries and they attract bass, pollack and coalfish between April and October. The cove on the east-facing side of **Start Point** is a very useful area for small-eyed ray. Fish to 16 lb are regularly taken on sandeel strip and peeler crab cocktails. In September and October brill is added to a long list of possible species.

Once past the Start Lighthouse the delights of **Lannacombe Bay** await. Drifting during middle range spring tides in a monthly pattern identical to the Skerries produces turbot, brill, plaice and dabs. Sport with bass is excellent and more double-figure fish are taken on driftlined flowing trace rigs than perhaps anywhere else within five miles of the coast. Big launce, large sandeels, can easily be feathered up for bait, although charter boats generally carry livebait tanks aboard.

Lannacombe has an attraction for John Dory, which are quite

rare in other parts of the South-West. Fish weighing 8 lb are often caught during high summer.

After an hour's run westward we come to the **East Rutts Reef**, which is a large area of thrusting pinnacles and canyons. Most of the fishing is done in late spring through to October, when pollack, cod, ling and bull huss are principal targets. Good conger are also frequently caught. A drawback are bait-stealing lesser spotted dogfish, which at times are an absolute menace.

This reef and the **West Rutts**, which is four miles farther down-Channel, are popular with private boat owners. Lying just outside the West Rutts is a wreck of some 7000 tons known as the **Coalboat**. It is well broken up and covers a large area of ground and, despite being fished for years, it remains a notable and productive mark.

Large pollack and coalfish come from it in winter and big conger still hide out in the maze of rusting plates and pipes. The spot is just over an hour's run from the Plymouth Sea Angling Centre and it can be found by using shore markers. There are eight small wrecks within five miles of the port and another three of fair size on the east side of the **Eddystone Reef**.

The small-boat angler can take good catches along the stretch of coast between **Bolt Tail** and the mouth of the **River Yealm**. The bottom is generally rocky, with large tracts of sand, ideal for bass two hours after dawn breaks.

Fishing around the **Mewstone Ledge** can be very productive if live sandeel is available for bait. There are two wrecks lying in **Bigbury Bay**, little more than a mile from the shore. They hold conger, while in autumn they are worth fishing for pollack.

Plymouth Sound offers the boat angler plenty of sport. Fishing close to the breakwater can be good for thornback ray and there are big conger lurking near the **Duke Rock buoy**, which is in the shadow of the towering Bovisand Cliffs. Driftlining at the 'bridge', which is in the gap between Drakes Island and Mount Edgcombe, can be worthwhile for bass during the big tides. Close by is **Barn Pool**, the deepest hole in the harbour. Strewn with old cables and a variety of junk, it makes a great conger eel lair.

Mike Millman

DEVON and CORNWALL

SHORE and boat-fishing tackle and techniques
are the same for both Devon and Cornwall, so
Mike Millman has combined them into one
expanded chapter.

Shore fishing tackle and techniques

THE coastline of Devon and Cornwall consists of storm beaches, headlands, long stretches of vaulting cliff, broken by small coves, many barely accessible, and estuaries behind which are miles of tidal river, and each needs to be tackled differently if the angler is to be successful.

A beach angler needs a rod capable of sending a 5½ oz lead, terminal tackle and bait at least 100 yards. A beginner will do best with a glass fibre rod some 12 feet long. The tip to middle section of the rod needs to be progressive to smooth out the jerky casting which is common among those new to beach fishing.

Once the art of casting has been mastered, and greater distance is the objective, it is time to perhaps move on to a much firmer rod, ideally made of carbon fibre, which features a stiffer tip action. This type of rod is fairly rigid up to about the second ring, where it begins to curve under compression. The power build is considerable and in experienced hands this type of rod is capable of casts well in excess of 150 yards.

Manufacturers of off-the-shelf rods tend to produce beachcasters that will suit the average angler. The keener fisherman is only happy with a rod custom-made, probably by a small specialist company headed by a top name in the casting world, or one built by himself, to exactly suit personal demands and physique.

Stiff action rods are best for lifting, a priority when conger fishing. A large eel is a stubborn beast and must be hauled away from its rocky habitat and kept moving towards the gaff. In this situation an all-through action beachcaster is next to useless.

There are two types of reel suitable for shore angling. The long-range caster generally prefers a multiplier reel correctly tuned so that line leaves it under minimum friction. Casts of 150 yards with terminal tackle and bait are possible with the right type of rod. Some multipliers are fitted with a cast control, which goes a long way to preventing the spool over-running, and line ending up in what is called a 'bird's nest'.

Constant practice is the only way to become a proficient caster, particularly if fishing after dark with a multiplier. Unless the rapidly revolving reel spool is checked with the thumb the instant the lead hits the water you're in for a frustrating untangling session! Top casters, who use the pendulum cast, can achieve incredible distances.

Fixed-spool reels are extensively used by beach anglers. Try to pick a make with a large, wide, not deep, spool. Models from the Shakespeare, Daiwa, Shimano and DAM companies hold about 250 yards of 30 lb line, a suitable breaking strain for West Country waters.

A word of warning here. Choose a fixed-spool reel with a spool-mounted drag system which can be screwed down tight before casting. A slipping spool can result in a cut finger, so it's best to avoid a rear setting clutch, which can never be fully locked down.

It is important to fill fixed-spool reels completely with line. If there's too much 'lip', casting distance will be reduced as line has to 'fight' its way over the edge of the rapidly emptying spool. Fixed-spool reels aren't suitable for tough situations, like conger fishing. In this case a stronger multiplier reel would be better.

Beach rods have either multiplier or fixed-spool rings which guide the line up the rod. Fixed-spool rings are larger and designed to cut down line friction during the cast. Line comes off the reel in a spiral and needs 'damping' down through a series of decreasing-diameter rings. Always specify which type of reel you intend using when buying a rod for beach fishing.

Nylon line is used for shore fishing. 12 to 20 lb line will cover most species likely to be found off a West Country beach, namely bass, cod, ray, whiting and flatfish. Where the ground is particularly rocky it's wiser to fish with 25 lb or even 30 lb line. Many anglers fishing for large wrasse and conger go even heavier, using 40 lb line to give a fair chance of hauling their catch ashore. Distance casting is not necessary in a rock fishing situation where there is deep water virtually under your feet, so strength and thickness of line is not so important from this point of view.

The most popular end rig for fishing a rocky or seaweed-covered seabed is the single-hook leger, with the lead being connected to

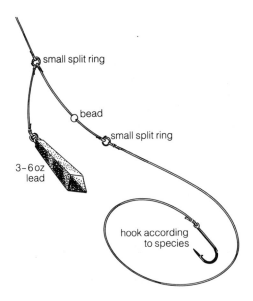

Figure 13 Shore casting rig for ray, bass, dogfish, turbot and plaice

the main trace via a weaker link of line. Connected by a small swivel placed above a bead, which has a cushioning effect if the lead becomes jammed, as it often does when rock fishing, a sharp tug will break the weak nylon, allowing the trace and perhaps a hooked fish to be retrieved. If you fish this rig ensure the trace is no longer than 18 inches in length.

A paternoster carrying one or two snoods to hooks, size depending on the species, is also effective, especially for long-distance work, although it is rarely used for conger fishing. For these big eels a single-hook leger trace 12 inches long and made up from 60 lb nylon or light wire is required. Hook size is usually 9/0 with an offset point. The lead is linked via a swivel to run on the reel line.

Beach casting can be dangerous. A lead weight breaking free during the cast could prove deadly and there are basic safety rules which must be followed. To minimise breaks use what is called a shock leader, very thick line which is generally just over double the length of the rod. As a general guide, for every ounce of lead cast match it with a line strength of 10 lb. For example, if you are fishing with a 5 oz sinker your leader should be 50 lb. The shock leader is connected to the main reel line with a leader or barrel knot, which should have at least six turns of nylon on each side to prevent slipping.

Connecting different thicknesses of line effectively together depends on the quality of the line. Cheap monofilament, which is often springy, isn't much good for tying complex knots. Shock leader knots stand proud and must always be positioned to the right of the spool, when fishing with a multiplier reel, otherwise the tag end can rip open your thumb as it revolves at high speed.

Tide and wind, or a combination of both, can play havoc with terminal gear. A grip lead with wire spikes is used to anchor tackle in the desired position, but it can be pushed out of position by the power of the tide and pulled round even farther by the wind catching the line. When this happens bite detection and effective striking becomes extremely difficult as the bow in the line puts you out of direct contact with the terminal tackle. The joys of beach fishing are indeed many!

Aim to cast behind the third breaker has long been a claim of beach anglers looking for such species as bass. It is true that fish are in this zone, but only when a gigantic surf is rolling on to the beach. In calmer conditions there is a better chance that the fish will be in the surf itself, where the disturbance is churning up food.

A classic example of how unpredictable fishing can be occurred during a competition held on Devon's Slapton beach. Most angler were casting a long way without success. Then a local angler with nearly 70 years' experience arrived and cast his bait, with outdated tackle, a relatively short way into the surf. The result was that, within the space of 60 minutes, he took four bass averaging 6 lb! It is a lesson well worth remembering.

Beach fishing is always best at night, especially for species like bass. On occasions the hunting fish will come into very shallow water and 10-pounders have been taken in less than a foot of water. This predator is most likely to be hunting during the flood tide; catch statistics show clearly that fishing at first light and at night is best.

On the beaches of Whitsands in south-east Cornwall, most of the big bass tend to be night captures. Bass are undoubtedly bolder after dark and will move much closer in to the beach. Rods are normally stood in a beach spike or in a tripod rod rest, although bite detection is often better if the rod is held. Failure to watch the rod-tip for that first signal of a bite could result in a lost fish. A bass feeds with a sideways slash, its body flank flat to the seabed. The fish should not be struck until it makes off in a mad dash, which often comes after a knock or two in quick succession on the rod top. After the hook has been set the rod is kept high and a tight line maintained to the fish.

In the dying moments of the fight wait until the sea has flattened and then net the fish. Trying to secure a bass by hand is simply asking to lose it and you could also end up with a badly lacerated hand, as the fish's gill-cover is razor sharp.

Trying to beach a fish is also foolish. Without its cushion of water it becomes heavier and, if caught by a large wave, the sudden movement and deadweight could break the line or tear the hook from the fish's mouth.

The majority of small-eyed, spotted and blonde ray taken by South-West anglers are hooked on leger rigs from rocky ledges and platforms some way above the sea which covers a sand or shingle bottom. The best fishing areas for these species tend to be sandy patches between outcrops of rock. A perfect example is Stoke Point, on the South Devon coast, where a very high proportion of the West's big specimens are caught; always after dark on live or frozen sandeel.

The first indication of a ray's interest in a bait is the slight movement of the rod top as the fish settles down over the bait. Always wait until the fish has got the bait in its mouth and moves off before striking. Because of the deep water and often difficult nature of the ground a wide-mouthed net with a 10-foot handle is needed to secure the fish. Roped drop nets are not suitable.

A conventional beach rod is widely used by ray anglers, although a more manageable, short outfit is better for fishing from ledges which are narrow and have a close-backing cliff. The 4–6 oz 9-foot uptide boat rod is now finding favour for rock fishing where distance doesn't matter.

Rocky ground is wrasse territory. The rougher and more lonely the mark, the better the chance of specimen-weight fish. It's a tough and uncompromising fish and you need a powerful rod and matching reel to gain the surprise advantage of pulling the fish those vital few feet away from ledges, gullies and deep holes which it will initially dive for. The ballan is a daylight species, at night it stays in a nest of weed deep in the rocks and refuses to feed. A single-hook leger carrying a 3/0 hook of stout construction is the best rig for taking the bigger fish from snaggy ground, but the paternoster is also very effective for working clean ground between rocks.

The sinuous conger eel, which is all power and muscle, is nocturnal. Find rocky ground and you will find the eels. Tidal rivers and harbours are highly productive and are best tackled with sturdy beach rods and single-hook leger rigs.

Float fishing is a very popular method for working rough ground under deep water. The sliding float rig is useful because the bait can be suspended at exactly the level the fish are feeding. This is achieved by fixing a rubber band or slider knot made from a short length of monofilament on the reel line.

Once the float hits the water it must stand vertically. If it doesn't the trace has tangled either during its flight or, more likely, it is lying on the bottom because the band was set too far up the line. The float is purely a means of getting a bait over otherwise inaccessible ground, like a thick bed of seaweed, where the fish will be hiding.

This sort of knowledge is very valuable, but it can only be gained by viewing the ground from a high cliff position when there is little water and a bright sun is showing the geography of the bottom. Rock anglers often draw sketch maps of favourite marks which show all the varied features at low water. The mark can then be fished productively when fully covered by the sea.

A heavy-duty spinning rod of around 10 feet long matched with a medium-sized fixed-spool reel filled with 20 lb line will prove perfect for float fishing.

The same rod and reel combination, but with a reduction in the line strength to around 15 lb, is an ideal outfit for pollack, which are often found feeding along the South-West coastline. For mullet, however, you really need a very light 10-foot rod with a soft action. If the rod is too stiff there's a danger of pulling your hook from the mullet's delicate mouth. Again, a small fixed-spool reel is ideal, only this time filled with 6 to 8 lb monofilament tied to a size 6 Aberdeen hook.

Floats for mullet fishing are very light and are cocked by a string of split shot. A stealthy approach, lots of groundbait, the swiftest of strikes at the slightest pull of the float and gentle patient playing are the rule to successful mullet fishing.

The art of spinning

BASS, pollack, coalfish and mackerel are predators with a great turn of speed. They prey on sandeel and small fish, including those of their own kind. The impulse to hunt and maim remains strong even when they are not hungry − a fact playing into the hands of an angler armed with a rod designed to flick a small metal lure or an artificial eel in their path.

Saltwater spinning rods range in length from seven to 10 feet and are available in glass fibre, graphite or mixes of these materials. Constant casting and retrieving, no matter how small the lure, is hard work, so the rod must be light and extremely well balanced if the technique is to be sustained over several hours.

A small fixed-spool reel holding about 200 yards of 8 lb line is the ideal tool for teaming with most spinning rods. Try to match the size and weight of any reel you buy with the length and weight of the rod you have.

The choice of metal blade lures is considerable, but many have little value — it is best to stick with those offered by the big name manufacturers for catching specific species. Vibration, rather than sight, is what draws a predator to the lure as it passes through the water, not gimmicks and colours!

A lure is designed to represent a swimming fish, perhaps injured, and, therefore, a tempting and easy target. The lure is kept moving every second it is in the water, otherwise it will sink like a stone. All too many anglers make the mistake of speeding up the retrieve and pulling the lure from the sea when it's still perhaps 20 feet from the casting position. Often a fish following the lure will be seen to turn away just as it is lifted out of the sea. Always work it right to your feet for the best chance of a take.

The heaviest metal lures can be cast without the need of additional weight, but this is not the case with the smaller lures and artificial eels, which must be lead-assisted to gain reasonable casting distance. There are two types of leads for this. One is the Jardine, a spiral of lead that has the line wrapped around it held in place by wires at both ends, and the other is the Wye, a banana-shaped sinker and a very traditional weight designed for spinning. Its shape means its centre of gravity is below the level of the line and this prevents it from twisting as the lure is drawn through the water.

Figure 14 Spinning rig

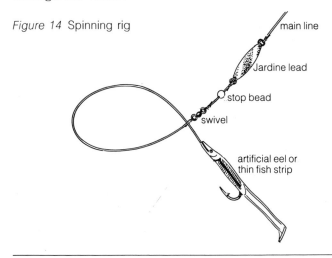

main line

Jardine lead

stop bead

swivel

artificial eel or thin fish strip

Spinning with a live sandeel is a deadly way of taking bass and pollack. The trace is constructed from 8 lb line, three feet in length, ending in a size 1 or 1/0 fine wire Aberdeen hook, with a needle-sharp point.

Crack of dawn is the best time to spin from rocks, piers and harbour walls. Always allow the lure or eel to sink for a few seconds before starting the retrieve. Then reel in steadily, perhaps occasionally speeding up, or slowing down, remembering to draw the lure as close to you as possible before lifting it out of the water.

The region's tidal rivers are full of flounder between October and late February providing steady and reliable sport when other species are far from land. A beachcaster capable of casting up to 6 oz of lead is used by most flounder anglers, who aim to drop their rigs into deep channels cut in the mud by tidal action.

The best feeding time is usually during the first two hours of the flooding tide. Before the water spills out across the mudflats fish are concentrated in the channels, so the likelihood of a bait being found and taken is much greater than later in the tide.

It is an advantage to know exactly where the middle of the channel is when the tide has covered it, so that terminal gear can still be cast into the right spot. A long stick driven into the mud during low tide acts as a marker and if it is long enough it will still show at the very top of the tide.

A single-hook leger or a two-hook paternoster is favoured by many flounder anglers, although it's a different story in Cornwall's tidal rivers, where a baited spoon is the killer rig. Flounder are very inquisitive fish and respond well to the spurts of mud kicked up along the bottom as the blade of the spoon works across it. Hooks are baited with lug, harbour rag, peeler crab or a tiny strip of squid.

During the early part of the flounder season, before the cold weather has set in, bait-robbing crabs can strip a hook clean in minutes. They can be beaten by incorporating a small balsa float, usually painted white, into the trace about six inches above the baited hook. This lifts the bait just far enough off the bottom to be out of the crab's way. Flounder have keen upward vision and can easily spot the bait wafting in the tide.

Boat fishing tackle and techniques

BOAT fishing off the South Devon and Cornish coasts can be divided into four categories, each demanding different tackle and techniques.

Harbours and tidal rivers can be very rewarding for the small-boat angler who gets things right. A double-handed spinning rod or a light uptider, small multiplier or fixed-spool reel have a starring role in encounters with bass, pollack and flatfish. A flowing trace, its length depending on the strength of tide, and a bait or artificial lure is the top-rated method for taking 'above the bottom' species.

Live prawn, which can be caught in a baited drop net fished at the bottom of harbour walls and close to the supports of piers after dark, is a deadly bait for shallow-water boat angling. Small live sandeels also have great catching capabilities.

Float fishing with a sliding rig is effective from an anchored boat in a good run of tide. It is, however, a much neglected method. The float is allowed to sweep away for up to 200 yards and is then worked slowly back to the boat. If the retrieve is too fast the baited hook will rise to the surface, which can be an advantage at times, but in the main most bass and pollack are caught close to the bottom.

It should be appreciated that the float technique is principally a method for fishing over ground which could not otherwise be worked effectively, for example wild water over rocks which would be dangerous to approach in a boat.

When a bite is felt which immediately comes to nothing, it is vital to keep winding slowly as this will often induce a second and more positive attack on the bait. This method of float fishing allows a great deal of ground to be covered, although the boat is not moving.

Legering with a single-hook rig is best for thornback, small-eyed, and blonde ray. Plaice, dabs and flounder also respond well to this technique. Wrasse are common in the rocky areas of most estuaries and tidal rivers, with a single-hook leger or a two-hook paternoster getting the best results.

An uptide rod is ideal for light bottom fishing. Heavier uptiders and conventional boat rods of 20 and 30 lb class should be used for conger, a species widely distributed close inshore. A multiplier reel built for rugged work is necessary, and a trace of commercial weight nylon or wire is needed as the fight with a sizeable eel, which has sharp teeth, could be lost before it has really begun if only light line is attached to the hook.

The chance of hooking a really heavy eel in tidal rivers and some harbours is enormous. Many big fish have been played to the side of a small boat, only to be cut free because the captor didn't want it in the boat with him!

Inshore boat fishing generally covers ground within five miles or so of the land. Boatcasting, the method whereby lead and bait are cast uptide with the aid of a light rod, is a popular inshore method, practised more up-channel. The do's, don'ts and undoubted advantages of uptiding are fully explained elsewhere in this guide (page 94). However, the method isn't greatly practised in the waters of the South-West, which are generally deep. In fact, it has been proved that boatcasting doesn't work in depths over 100 feet.

An uptide rod, however, can be used to tackle turbot, plaice, dabs, the many types of ray and cod, which feed on the bottom, and for bass, pollack, and coalfish above it. Alternatively, a light seven-foot conventional boat rod is perfectly suitable.

Bass and pollack anglers rely heavily on a flowing trace technique called a 'flying collar'. There is nothing to touch it when using live sandeel, artificial eels, thin strips of squid, mackerel or king ragworm. During the early part of the year king ragworm is a deadly bait, particularly for pollack, and many anglers put the worms on a hook which has previously been tied with a few whispy feathers.

A short length of bicycle valve tubing is first run on to the trace, which is then connected to the eye of the hook. The feathers are then whipped on with cotton and glued. When dry the tube is eased down over the eye and shank. Prepared at home, this little trick can put a lot of pollack on the hook during the day.

The 'collar rig' centres around a wire boom about eight inches long which is swivelled at points A and B, the weight being attached at C. Swivels and carrier are attached to the wire with split rings. The length of the boom ensures that the trace, which can be up to 20 feet long, is standing well clear of the reel line on its way to the bottom in the tide. Only when the water is flowing fast enough to carry the trace well out can the rig be dropped at fair speed.

A thumb controls the speed of the spool. Once bottom is reached a steady retrieve is begun and the reel turns are counted, so that the feeding level may be established. Once it is, the dead ground can be worked through quickly. Pollack and bass usually dive deep and very fast after taking the bait, and if the reel clutch is not set correctly to suit the strength of line being used a break is almost certain. Fish must be able to take line under pressure.

If a 'pluck' at the bait is detected during the slow retrieve keep the reel turning at exactly the same speed. If a second take also comes to nothing wait for a second or two and then wind fast, which often induces a firm attack. Moving the eel or bait very fast is sometimes the only way to get a fish on the hook. The vibration it creates incites an attack.

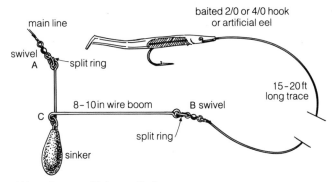

main line

baited 2/0 or 4/0 hook
or artificial eel

swivel
A

split ring

15-20ft
long trace

8-10in wire boom

B swivel

C

split ring

sinker

Figure 15 West Country 'flying collar'

Artificial eels come in a multitude of colours, and the names to look for are Eddystone, Red Gill and Delta, which are widely used over rough ground and wrecks. Black lures have a fine big fish catching record, followed by luminous yellow. Why colours so far apart have such a high level of attraction will probably remain a mystery.

Store artificial eels carefully in your tackle box. Ensure the tails do not become kinked or distorted, as this reduces vibration, the reason the lures work in the first place.

The long trace rig is always used to fish live sandeels, which can swim about quite naturally tethered to 12 lb line. To mount a live eel, pass the hook point of an Aberdeen through the sandeel's mouth and then nick it into the skin just behind the head on the underside of its body. In a slow tide situation you could hook the eel through the skin just behind the top of the head.

The 'flying collar' set-up is also used to search the bottom for flatfish, although the trace is kept tight and lowered to the seabed. Failure to do this allows the tide to lift the bait off the bottom and out of a fish's reach.

An uptide rod in the 4 to 6 oz class matched with a medium-sized multiplier, preferably with a level-wind facility, filled with 15 lb line is an excellent combination for taking on the tasty turbot. This is a species principally found on the offshore sand-banks, like the Skerries off Dartmouth. These giant flatfish tend to lie in hollows and depressions created by the tide scour, where they wait for food to be swept within reach.

The turbot has a mouth like a steel trap which can open through a series of hinged flaps to an incredible size. It also possesses amazing speed and can rise out of the sand, grab its victim or bait and be back on the bottom in a flash. The 'take' of a turbot transmits powerfully to the rod tip, which kicks two or three times in rapid succession. The rod should be lifted firmly to ensure a good hook hold, but it is a mistake to strike hard, for the turbot's hinged mouth is soft and easily tears. If the hook lodges in a soft area the fish will probably be lost.

The species is a great and crafty fighter, using the power of the tide and an arching body to try to escape. Its powerhouse of a tail gives it tremendous propulsion and it makes long runs which test both tackle and angler. Line will be taken off the reel constantly and no attempt should be made to get it back until the fish has finished swimming. Then it must be pumped to the surface with patience and smoothness. Most turbot come to the surface well downtide of an anchored boat and must then be drawn to the waiting net with great care.

Beware of the turbot's final rush for freedom and remember to slacken off the reel's clutch in the dying moments of the fight so that your line doesn't break.

The majority of turbot caught from sandbanks are taken on strips of sandeel, which are cut from the fish with a very thin long-bladed knife, cocktails of squid strip and peeler crab, razorfish and marine worm. Oddly enough, although the live sandeel is one of the staple foods for turbot it is not a great hook bait used whole. A thin strip of meat is much better.

Turbot tactics also catch plaice, which are best caught on light tackle. Local anglers with long experience use an uptide-type rod and small multiplier filled with 10 lb line. The trace, which should be of the same weight or a little lighter as the main line, is long and carries a size 1 or 1/0 hook. It is worked off a boom which carries a weight or is sent down by a ball lead positioned behind the trace swivel.

Plaice are very inquisitive fish and half a dozen small, brightly coloured beads, preferably of the day-glow variety, are placed above the hook as an additional attractor. A small Mepps or similar metal lure can be positioned about eight inches above the hook to catch a fish's attention.

The best West Country bait for plaice is a cocktail of peeler crab, a couple of very thin strips of squid and a lugworm. Combinations of razor fish, hermit crab, mussel and the baits already mentioned can all be successful. Live sandeel or strips of eel do not do very well, although this little fish is an important link in the flattie's food chain.

Plaice take a bait with a very cautious pluck, but it can be detected on a sensitive rod-tip. Once spotted, a couple of feet of line should be slackened away. Moments later there should be a more determined attack and this is when the rod is lifted to set the hook. There's no need to tear the fish's head off, although it is hard getting this message across to inexperienced anglers.

Dabs are often hooked during plaice fishing sessions and their presence is often heralded by a series of rattles on the rod-tip. Dabs are, despite their small size, spirited little fighters and on very light tackle give grand sport.

They can also be fished for with a two- or three-hook paternoster in conventional form with the sinker at the bottom, although it's better to have the lead above the swivel to give the trace snoods, which should be about 10 inches long, freedom to move. When this style is used the bottom hook is connected to the body of the rig and the snoods evenly spaced along its three-and-a-half foot length. Size 1 fine wire hooks, with two or three small beads above them, should be used. 12 lb line is ideal for tying up this rig.

A traditional method for catching dabs is to use a spreader rig. Closely resembling a coat-hanger, but fashioned out of much lighter but stiffer wire, it is eyed at the central point and at the end of each arm. Split rings connect tiny swivels to which are attached three-foot-long mono traces carrying size 1 hooks. The reel line connects to the eye in the middle of the wire and the weight is placed above the swivel.

Reef fishing

FISHING the offshore reefs lying in fairly deep water is a popular sport. Most South-West reefs are within a two-hour run of the charter fishing ports, a principal reason why so many anglers take this type of trip.

An area of rough ground, perhaps with pinnacles of rock thrusting vertically towards the surface, but still with 100 feet of water over them, are a great attraction for fish of many kinds. It's an eat and be eaten world with only the shark, and perhaps the biggest of conger and skate, enjoying a safe life, with the only threat being man. In this category of boat fishing we find pollack, cod, ling, dogfish and whiting in considerable numbers, and at times there's also pack tope and spurdog to provide a thrilling alternative.

Seasons have a big bearing on what's swimming over a reef, although some fish are in residence all year round, notably conger, ling and members of the dogfish family. Reef fishing takes its toll on tackle, so buy the best rod and reel you can afford to cover most of the situations and species likely to be found. Until fairly recently the rod would have been a 20 lb class pole rather shorter than seven feet and made in two pieces, the unbroken tip section fitting into a butt with a quality screw winch fitting.

This type of rod is still quite suitable, although some boat anglers are now switching to the uptider or boatcasting rod, as it is sometimes called. Averaging about nine feet long, it is ideal for conventional boat fishing, especially aboard a crowded charter craft. Fishing away from the favoured stern position with this type of rod is no longer a disadvantage, since you can fish outside the anglers further down the boat, and your terminal tackle will head for the bottom through clear water. With the shorter rod you could spend half the day untangling your gear from everybody else's down your side of the boat.

A 4–6 oz uptider will, in fact, handle up to 8 oz of lead in what can be termed a straight 'up and down' fishing pattern. Rarely will more lead be needed when using 20 lb line, since it has a fine diameter and is very strong.

A multiplier reel in the 4/0 class, or slightly smaller, with or without a level-line facility matches well. The benefits of a multi- plier with a lever-drag mechanism as opposed to the traditional star-drag system cannot be overstated. The easily adjusted lever allows fine tuning of the clutch as a fish is played to the surface and the additional cost of the reel will be quickly rewarded once you have a good fish on the end of the line.

The next class of rod for reef fishing is the 30 lb rated model. Having good lifting power, linked with a good action, it is right for bringing conger, ling and heavy cod to the gunwale.

A two-and-a-half-foot leger rig made up of 100 lb line carrying a single 9/0 hook is used almost exclusively for rough ground conger. The eels seldom attack a bait fiercely. Most mouth it, drop it, move around and pick it up again. When the first touch is felt a yard of line is let out, which gives the fish a little extra moving space. A hard tug followed immediately by a second pull is a fair indication that the bait has been accepted.

Reefing for conger is a slow game and the wise angler rests his rod against the gunwale, the reel out of gear but with the ratchet on, and holds the line between thumb and forefinger, feeling for every movement down below.

To hook a fish, reel in the slack line slowly until you are in direct contact with the trace and fish. If the conger has taken the bait properly, it will immediately back away and the rod will register tension. This is the moment to strike with a smooth sweep instantly followed by a rapid pumping and winding action. A belly pad acts as the anchoring point of the rod butt, and also protects the stomach from bruising.

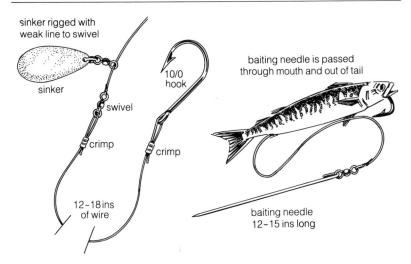

Figure 16 Conger rig baited with whole mackerel

The element of surprise should win 20 feet of line and pull the fish clear of the bottom. Failure to work swiftly and hard in these vital first seconds could lose you the fish. A conger of only 30 lb is a mass of powerful muscle and it will try to dive into a convenient hole or wrap its body around rocks. Breaking the hold is difficult and at times impossible. If your conger has taken hold a good trick is to slacken off all the tension and wait. The eel may just decide that the danger is past and move off, giving you a second chance to get it clear. The scenario is from an anchored boat.

Reef-caught ling tend to weigh less than 20 lb. The best way to catch them is with a paternoster tied from a single length of 40 lb line. Tie a blood-loop knot large enough to form a six-inch double snood. Ling have very sharp teeth and the double thickness of line is some security should a big specimen attach itself.

Ling are ravenous feeders and hit a bait hard and fast. No skill is required – just hang on! Bite, strike and haul 'em up is the sequence, although doing this time after time can become tiring and very boring. Best bait for reef conger is mackerel, squid or cuttlefish. If you're after ling send down any kind of fish bait, because the species is a dustbin.

For whiting and pouting tackle up with a light paternoster armed with size 1 or 1/0 hooks. Pollack and coalfish respond best to the 'flying collar' rig, a technique described earlier. Many cod are taken by the same method, or on a ling outfit.

Nylon fishing line, which has much less resistance to tide flow than other types of line, with the sole exception of wire, should be used for all deep-water work.

Wire line has the finest tide-cutting qualities and also gives maximum bite detection, although it should only be used when everybody else aboard is fishing with wire. Nylon and wire shouldn't be mixed because the wire will quickly slice through every nylon line it touches. A quality wire line doesn't come cheap, which puts some anglers off using it, which is a pity because it can bring so many benefits.

Wire line is best used on a narrow-diameter multiplier reel that has a metal spool, while the rod must have roller rings and a roller tip to take the friction and wear. Best roller rings are Aftco and Micas.

Wrecking – West Country style

WRECK fishing many miles from land is the toughest category of boat angling. The demands it can make on the angler have already been described, now it's the tackle's turn to come under scrutiny.

The majority of offshore wreck sites visited by South-West-based charter boat skippers, lie rusting in deep water. 40 fathoms is about average and another 10 on that can be encountered without venturing into the trench zone off the Channel Islands, where half as much again is found.

Deep water means strong tides and as the gear is heading for the bottom, pressure on the line sweeps it far from the vertical. The bait eventually reaches bottom a long way behind an anchored boat. All too often there is the situation where an angler, without experience of deep-water fishing, is unprepared for the depth and tide and can't get his tackle and bait anywhere near the wreck. Unless he can beg, borrow or steal more line and a bigger reel, the day will be a waste of time.

At the very least a 4/0 multiplier reel carrying more than 400 yards of 35 lb line is needed – and it must be top-quality gear. Bigger fish are found over offshore wrecks and the reel's clutch mechanism must be capable of withstanding the great and repetitive pressure. Clutch failure, and the inability to winch a fish up, is very common and many cheaper multipliers can't stand the pace and mechanisms quickly jam or fail. I have seen it happen with a brand new reel when its owner was bringing up his first heavy ling!

Still standing head and shoulders above all others for wreck fishing are the Penn Senator 4/0 and 6/0 reels, but be prepared to part with a lot of cash. They are not cheap. For fishing against tough but smaller species like pollack, coalfish and cod, Sigma, Mitchell and ABU multipliers are widely used.

These fish can be taken successfully on a 20 lb class rod, although hardened boat anglers prefer a 30 lb model with its superior lifting power. If you use light tackle from a crowded charter boat you won't get admiring looks, particularly after you have tangled up with the angler nearest to you and perhaps all those on your side of the boat. It has been known for offenders to have a sharp knife passed across their line!

Modern boat rods tend to be seven feet long, which is fine for off-the-bottom species, but not so good for hauling heavy conger and ling. For these a six-and-a-half-foot, 30 lb rod with a firm action and good lifting ability is vital. A long rod, with a soft action, gives little chance of hauling a conger away from the bottom quickly.

Sheer lifting power is the key to successful wrecking, but don't rush off and buy a broom stick. Many wreck anglers have 20 lb, 30 lb and 50 lb rods available on a trip and switch around between the outfits through the day as conditions dictate.

There are three basic techniques in wreck fishing; legering with a heavy-duty trace of mono or wire line carrying a single 10/0 hook for conger, ling and perhaps cod; the 'flying collar' rig with the reel line stepped up to around 25 lb and the trace to 20 lb for pollack, coalfish, cod and bream; and 'killer gear', a tough

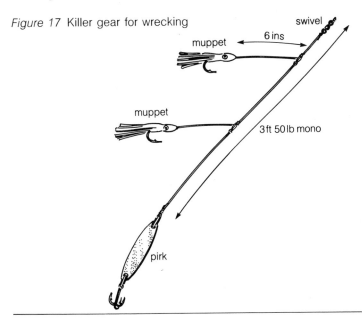

Figure 17 Killer gear for wrecking

paternoster carrying two six-inch snoods connected to artificial eels, for taking free-swimming species.

The sinker is usually a pirk weighing about 26 oz, which is baited with mackerel or squid. The gear is worked from a 30 lb stiff-action rod and a multiplier with a high retrieve. Some anglers, particularly those with stamina, use a 50 lb rod. The gear is allowed to plummet to the wreck and if the eels are not taken before it gets there the rig is retrieved with a series of jerks up to about 100 feet above the wreckage. If still no takes, the whole process is repeated.

It is not unusual for a couple of outsize pollack or coalfish to hit the eels simultaneously and for a ling to hang itself on the pirk. Only the best tackle can cope with this crude but highly efficient method.

Finally comes the conventional paternoster carrying two or three snoods and artificial eels or 4/0 to 6/0 baited hooks. A bomb-type weight is used to get the rig down to ling, cod and to a lesser extent pollack and 'coalies'. On a wreck likely to be carrying a good head of big fish it is unwise to stretch to more than three hooks — hauling four or five fish to the surface at once would be an almost impossible task.

Figure 18 Two-hook paternoster armed with artificial eels for wrecking

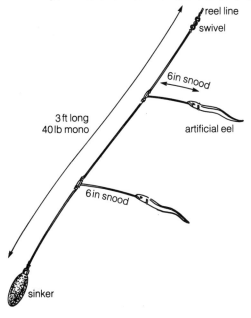

Sharks – the ultimate test

SHARK fishing isn't restricted to the big-game resorts of the Caribbean – they can be caught in British waters as well, and especially in the West Country.

Sharking, particularly for blues, in the lower English Channel is from a drifting boat with up to four baits fished at the same time, all at different depths, the first at 30 feet down, the next at 60 feet, the third at 100 feet and the last really deep at 130 feet, the idea being to fish as much water as possible until a shark is found. Mackerel, pilchard and fresh herring are the most common baits and they are suspended from colourful balloon floats, which can easily be spotted bobbing about in the troughs when there is a fair swell running.

Mackerel is used whole with its backbone removed from behind the head to the tail to allow its juices to seep out in the tide. It is mounted on a 10/0 forged offset hook attached to a 15-foot wire or heavy-duty mono trace. The length of the trace is vital because sharks have a habit of rolling up a trace and winding it around their bodies. If the reel line comes into contact with their sandpaper-like skin the fish is instantly lost.

The trace is swivelled at the half-way point and, of course, where it connects with the reel line. The depth of the bait is set by tying a rubber band, which is connected to the balloon, tight to the line. An alternative, and much simpler method, is to use a plastic flat-sided clip which can be secured tight to the reel line. It

Figure 19 Shark rig

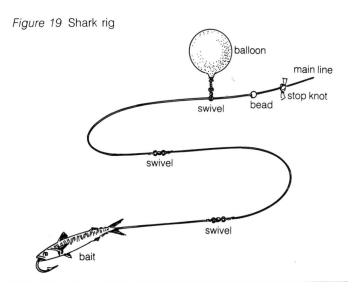

is lightly wired to a water cistern ball-cock, also made of plastic. It takes but a second to release the clip, allowing the float rig to fall back to the trace swivel, where it comes within reach at the conclusion of the fight.

When a shark picks up a bait all the other rigs are wound in out of the way. No attempt should be made to strike the fish until it has had time to turn and swallow the bait, which it always does in an upside down position. Several yards of line must be stripped off the reel the instant the bite is detected to give the fish time to chew the bait.

The blue, in particular, is quite a canny fish, and will all too easily let go if it is suspicious. When it begins its second run there is a fair chance the bait has been taken properly and now is the time to strike home the hook with a series of strong and swift lifts of the rod. A blue in the 75 lb plus class is a rough customer and certainly in the early stages must be played with patience.

It has the power to run fast and long, which can strip line off a multiplier reel at an alarming rate. The clutch must be set to give line under tension which will gradually and, hopefully, wear the fish out. Line is gained by a steady pumping action. The rod is then raised and the fish lifted. This drill is repeated until the shark reaches gloved hands. On no account is the reel handle turned when the fish is running.

A belly pad should be worn to protect the stomach from bruising. Most shark boats have a fighting chair, but it takes a lot of the fun out of the game.

A 30 lb class rod matched with a 4/0 multiplier reel loaded with the appropriate weight of line is quite adequate for dealing with even a big blue, provided you don't try to hassle it.

The much bigger porbeagle shark, which is not all that common in the waters off the Channel coast of Cornwall, can occasionally be caught and much heavier tackle is needed to beat them. A 50 lb class rod and 6/0 multiplier filled with 50 lb line will give you a better chance of coming out the victor. A high percentage of porbeagles weigh 150 lb plus, and giants in world record class, which is 465 lb, come from the waters in the Bude Bay area of Atlantic Cornwall and at Hartland Point, which is 15 miles farther up the coast.

On either side of the Cornish peninsula the best chance of a porbeagle is close in to the cliffs, where there is deep water, and over the offshore reefs such as the Eddystone and Hands Deeps, where this top predatory species likes to prey on pollack, ling and cod. The giant mako and thresher sharks are also found in Cornish waters from time to time.

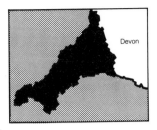

Devon

Mike Millman

CORNWALL

Lamorna Cove — typical mullet and bass country

CORNWALL, with its rugged coastline, is a sea angler's paradise. The deep, clear waters are the home of some of the hardest-fighting fish to be found in British waters. Mike Millman pinpoints where the fish can be found.

CORNWALL – A SEPARATE COUNTRY?

IT is often claimed that Cornwall is a country in its own right. A peninsula jutting out into the Atlantic, its softer south coast is washed by the English Channel for over 100 miles from the Tamar River to the cliffs of Land's End.

Cornwall is renowed for its mix of firm, golden sand beaches and high cliffs ablaze in summer with wild flowers. At the eastern end of the county is the magnificent panorama of Whitsand Bay arching between Rame Head and Looe. When the tide falls back there is an unbroken seven-mile stretch of the finest sand, popular with both holidaymakers and beach fishermen. Many a bass angler heads for the beach here, clutching rod and tackle bag on the walk down the cliff path. On a dark night lamps glowing as far as the eye can see are a testament to the attraction of Whitsands.

Atop the great headland of Rame is a tiny chapel dedicated to mariners. It has been a landmark for over 1000 years and similar buildings of granite can be found along the coastline. Further west can be seen the remains of 18th- and 19th-century tin and copper mines. Abandoned engine houses, with stacks still standing proud, cling almost impossibly to the cliffs.

Kings have left their stamp on the county. The great castle of Pendennis, built by Henry VIII, guards the western entrance to Falmouth and on its eastern flank is the small St Mawes castle, regarded as one of the best examples of Tudor fortification. Off Marazion is St Michael's Mount, a granite island topped by an inhabited castle dating back to the 12th century. The view of the coast is breathtaking from the castle and, weather and tide permitting, it is reached on foot across a cobbled causeway.

All of Cornwall's principal ports are on the comparatively sheltered Channel coast. Falmouth is well established as a repair yard for big ships and it's not unusual for large liners to dominate the skyline. Par is one of the busiest harbours in Europe. Around the clock, coasters collect Cornwall's white gold – china clay which is dug and washed from the ground around the St Austell area.

Newlyn is the principal fishing port, being closest to the open Atlantic. Before the continental shelf finally ends in an abrupt abyss there are many sea-mounts rising out of very deep water which hold many varieties of fish. From these reefs, which are beyond the reach of anglers, come conger, ling, cod and pollack that put rod records to shame.

There are several dozen smaller fishing villages, some at the western end beyond Penzance, lying behind little more than a cleft in a cliff of granite. These have changed little across the years, and everyday small fleets of boats skippered by men who have never known any other way of life, sail in the quest for mackerel, pollack, bass, lobster and crab.

This most westerly section of the Channel coast has very high cliffs and the waterline can only be reached in a few places. The South West Peninsula Coast Path follows the entire 272 miles of the Cornish coastline and gives the opportunity to view the spectacular scenery. The Cornish coast is treacherous and many offshore lighthouses warn mariners of the dangers. Westerly gales are frequent, especially in the lower end of the Channel, and heavy seas have been known to reach lantern level at the Bishop Rock, Longships and Wolf Lights.

Beneath the surface from the Eddystone all the way down-channel the geography is unique. Numerous great reefs covered by deep water lying within ten miles of the coast provide happy hunting grounds for commercial and sport anglers. In this widest part of the English Channel tides do not run fast, but a fair number of fishing days are lost to strong winds.

Cornwall has a very mild climate. In the far west palm trees and other semi-tropical shrubs and plants are quite common. Snow occasionally falls over the region, but the deposits are light and rarely last long in the salt air. The county's weather pattern is very changeable. A gale one day can be replaced by a flat calm the next. In the far west there are more hours of sunshine each year than in any other part of Britain and Penzance is rated as one of the top holiday sunshine towns.

There is a land beyond Cornwall. 28 miles to the south-west are the Isles of Scilly. Washed by the Gulf Stream, this maze of islands, islets and rocky outcrops enjoys a sub-tropical climate which can be compared in some ways with the Mediterranean.

Flowers are the main industry and in January and February, when the mainland is cloaked in a grey mantle, the Scillies are a blaze of colour from daffodils and narcissi, which are exported to Europe. The five inhabited islands are served by launches which operate daily from St Mary's, but winter gales quite often cut off the islands of Tresco and St Martins.

There is good shore fishing and it's never difficult to take a big wrasse or two from deep-water gullies. Mullet are numerous all around the islands, while spinning will take pollack, mackerel and garfish. There is some opportunity for boat fishing and the most popular area is the Bishop Rock Reef. Lying just outside the Western rocks, the ground fishes well for pollack. The Scillies are reached by ship or helicopter from Penzance or by air from Plymouth and Newquay.

Shore fishing guide to Cornwall's south coast

CROSS the River Tamar into Cornwall and the first fishing venue we are met with is **Cremyl**, on the west side of the river, a noted spot for thornback ray, which start to arrive during April, or earlier if the weather is mild.

Most of the fishing at Cremyl is from the small beach to the left of the ferry slipway. On the right side is rougher ground under a fortification from the Napoleonic period. Thornback heading upstream are found in a deep channel worn by fast tides and an 80-yard cast is needed to put the bait, usually peeler crab, in the right place. Sizeable conger are taken here, but the ground can only be fished during neap tides. The two hours to high water late in the evening is probably the best time.

The **Tamar** is a fine flounder river and at its best between October and late February. The shoreline at **Palm Rock**, which is at the entrance to Millbrook Creek, is a popular venue and the harbour wall, directly opposite at South Down, is also worth a try for flatfish. Nearby is **St John's Lake**, which is also a top flounder spot, especially in December and January, when fish in the 4 lb class can be expected.

An area of considerable merit and the first fronting the open sea is **Penlee Point**. The access road from Kingsand is now only for those having business at the Coastguard station, so it's a walk of just over a mile along a wooded lane to reach the spot. The mark is at its best for bass just as dawn breaks and at times working late in the evening can be successful. A big tide is preferred and live sandeel are quite clearly the best bait. This is excellent wrasse territory, especially on the south side of the Point, catches hitting a peak after July.

Conger are plentiful, but the rough terrain plays into the fishes' favour and many are lost. It is sound to examine the ground at low water so that the more open spaces between the rocks can be mapped. They show quite clearly in bright conditions. Penlee can be reached by driving up the lane which is just before Rame Church. About a mile later there's open ground on which to park.

The Looe River and Banjo Pier

The fishing harbour of Mevagissey

The Point is now a quarter of a mile below.

Rame Head dominates the East Cornish coast. Its base is a jumbled mass of broken rock, deep mysterious gullies with a covering of kelp and two large lagoons when the tide is in. A path swinging left at the stile below the Coastguard lookout station leads to rocky platforms above deep water. In one spot, when the tide is low, spider crabs can usually be seen clinging to the sheer walls of a cleft holding many feet of water. Under its overhangs are wrasse.

To the right of the Head a series of paths meander down a steep cliff thick with gorse. It takes about 15 minutes to reach the waterline, but the effort can be worthwhile. There is a choice of rocky ledges projecting some way out and the wrasse fishing is excellent. Divers have reported fish in the 10 lb class hiding under overhangs and in deep holes. Would-be record-breakers take note.

Queener Point, which is to the right, is an ideal spot for bass fishing with a sliding float rig carrying live sandeel or prawn bait. Early morning and late evening is the time to expect action during summer and autumn. 'Queeners' faces beautiful Whitsand Bay with its almost endless surf beach of fine sand broken by rock into named areas. **Happy Valley**, **Main Beach**, **Tregonhawke**, **Freathy** and **Tregantle** all give bass, but rarely in daylight. The whole of the area is good for small-eyed ray, which respond best to live sandeel, but only after dark. Live eels can be scraped or dug from the sand at the water's edge.

Close to Freathy is the **Grotto**, a narrow outcrop of rock which stretches well out from the cliff. Bass, turbot, ray and plaice are taken during the summer and autumn and it's a good winter mark for big pollack. The Grotto gets its name from a cavern carved out of the living rock by a gout sufferer in the 1800s. Its walls carry rhymed messages.

A very good bass beach is right under the Whitsand Bay Hotel at **Portwrinkle**. Leger gear carrying crab or a mixed bait cocktail lobbed on to the clear sand between the rock outcrops after dark during a spring tide can do wonders. Proof that the bass is not an exclusive night feeder; two scaling over 12 lb were caught in bright daylight at Tregantle.

The beaches at **Seaton** and **Downderry** have also yielded double-figure bass and the best at the former is a 13½-pounder, which took a peeler crab and worm cocktail bait. They are mostly fished for at night during a rising spring tide. In cold winters coalfish averaging about 1½ lbs provide steady sport in this area.

Banjo Pier, Looe, can only be used by anglers during the winter, due to the town's great popularity as a holiday resort. It's a fine spot for ambushing flounder as they make their way upstream through the very narrow gap. Double-figure pollack have been hooked in January on big legered baits, especially squid head. Directly opposite under **Hannafore** is **White Rock**, so called because of a white splash of paint. It forms the western entrance to the river and harbour. Large wrasse are often taken here in the warm months; the best recorded scaled over 7 lb. Mullet are reasonably plentiful along the Hannafore stretch from April on and fall to bread and mackerel flake offered on sliding float gear. Specialists groundbait the forward rocks at low tide and work back with the water. Early morning sessions pay the best dividends. Just offshore is the privately owned **Looe Island**. Visitors are allowed during the summer and regular trips are operated by small boats from Looe. The mullet fishing is very good indeed and several 6-pounders are reported every year. The seaward side tends to be largely inaccessible.

Polperro, a few miles down the coast, is the most painted and photographed fishing village in England, and it becomes very crowded during the summer. Fishing is mostly for mackerel and garfish with a float during warm evenings when the tide is well up. There are numerous rocky spots for wrasse some way to the east and west of the tiny harbour.

Stinker Cove, so called because of the rotting weed after winter storms, is a typical rock fishing mark for wrasse, pollack and conger. It's also good mullet ground, the fish being attracted by maggots living among the weed fronds. Groundbait should be a mixture of fish and bread laced with pilchard oil.

Talland Sands is good for bass after dark. Squid and cuttlefish are recommended baits and should be cast on to the sandy patches between the rocks. There are plenty of wrasse in the area and conger are on the move after dark. A stiff climb and tramp down a much overgrown path leads to **Colors Cove**. This little-visited spot has tremendous potential for very big wrasse and good pollack also hunt along this wild stretch. It's the sort of mark to arrive at in daylight, fish through the night and leave when it is light.

Lansallos, where the coastal path cuts in from Lansallos Church and runs along the cliffs above a rocky stretch of coast, is quite capable of yielding double-figure wrasse. The gullies are still covered by deep water at low tide and once it begins to make the fish come on the feed. One of the best catches in a day is a 37-fish haul, with most scaling over 4 lb, the best 6¾ lb. All were taken on legered peeler crab. Mullet are all along this stretch and at times fair-size shoals move in the coves. June to October is the best period for mullet between Looe and Fowey. Most fish are caught in the early morning.

Fowey has been an angling mecca for generations. Mullet abound during the summer in the harbour area and penetrate far into the tidal river. On the east side is **Polruan**, where there is deep water right out to the estuary mouth. Sliding float tackle baited with worm, crab or live prawn takes wrasse, mackerel, pollack and mullet. Close by is **Pont Creek**, which is a good area once the tide starts to make for school bass and mullet. In summer when the trees, which sweep right down to the water's edge from high ground, are in full leaf, the silence and setting is idyllic. In winter the Fowey is a superb flounder river offering specimens up to 4 lb and possibly bigger. The railway goods siding, which is reached by a waterside path from the village of **Golant**, is an excellent spot from which to cast on to sandbars stretching across the river. Flounder will be on the sheltered side, depending which way the tide is flooding, and a baited spoon rig cast across and then retrieved at a steady pace stands a fine chance of being taken. This stretch of the river also gives bass, but the number entering the Fowey is much reduced these days. Huge conger hole up in the Fowey and a good many in the 40 lb class have been taken from the shoreline. A very useful spot is the **Bodinnick Ferry Slipway**, from where a 60-yard cast will place a leger bait in more than a 100 feet of water. A neap tide is essential to fish the neck.

Crinnis Beach at Carlyon Bay shelves steeply at the western end and is often washed by a good surf. Sandeel are taken by the thousand in commercial nets and end up frozen in packets for anglers. It follows that this is bass territory and many fish are taken in the first hours of daylight, mostly during spring tides. Plaice, dabs and flounder often feature in winter catches and at times there is good whiting and coalfish fishing. Crinnis is a holiday beach and best avoided during summer days. A couple of miles away is the small working harbour of **Charlestown**, now privately owned and undergoing development, which will surely change its face with the possibility of restricted fishing. It has a substantial outer harbour wall giving easy float and bottom fishing. Work from half-tide up at the break of day. Mullet used to be numerous here, but catches have fallen away badly, possibly due to intensive netting in this area. On both sides of the harbour there are rocky zones holding wrasse. Conger to 38 lb have been hooked at night.

Porthpean offers beach fishing at first and last light for bass. The last two hours to the top of the tide and first hour back is reckoned to give the best chance. This is usually a worthwhile mark after a gale has churned up the bottom, exposing razorfish and other food. **Pentewan** should be fished during the second half of the flood tide. It's a first-light beach and live sandeel is the best bait. A reasonable mark for flounder in the late summer and autumn.

Port Giskey is principally a wrasse station, best on the flood tide. A very rough bottom and heavy weed encourages sliding float fishing, but the method does not get the specimens. One or two notable bass have been taken here. The best baits include razorfish and sandeel. **Poistreath** can produce bass during the rising tide at first-light, which is also a good time to lay a light float rig for mullet. Conger become active after dark over the flanking rocky areas. Squid, cuttlefish and big cocktails, including king ragworm, have proved successful.

Mevagissey is a bustling holiday town with a fairly big commercial fishing industry. Its outer harbour wall is a popular spot for float fishing, which takes mackerel, garfish and pollack. Raw beginners have had the luck to catch large bass from the lighthouse end and Cornwall's shore record fish weighing 14 lb 2 oz had its origins here. It went for a whole squid head legered after dark for conger. A two-mile hike via **Portmellon** takes you to **Chapel Point**, one of the top areas in Cornwall for large wrasse. Fish to 10¼ lb, which is considerably heavier than the British record, have reliably been taken and 6-pounders are fairly common. One of the best catches was three over 7 lb in a tide, taken by a holiday visitor. Between the Point and **Turbot Point** there is good rough ground and excellent fishing, although, despite its name, there are no turbot these days. **Pabyer Point** also offers the chance of big wrasse and sliding float fishing with prawn can be good for pollack. Late in the autumn and through the winter there is a fair run of good-sized fish.

Gorran Haven is a pretty village loved by summer tourists. It has accessible rocky ground which can be fished with a sliding float. Most of the popular species show from time to time and there are certainly big conger in the area. A few years ago a monster of 120 lb was taken on a longline set just 400 yards offshore from the harbour. Live prawn on a float rig are the top-rated bait for bass. The coastline running around to the Dodman Point is mostly of rock with a few beaches. Pollack, wrasse, bull huss and conger are the principal species to be expected. In the depths of winter there could be very good whiting fishing along this stretch and the sandy ground could well hold ray.

Dodman Point is a dangerous area and even rock fishing

experts experience difficulty reaching the water in places. The jagged mass of rock holds large wrasse and pollack that could undoubtedly be taken from the shore judging by the big fish caught closein by commercial fishermen. No shortage of sizeable conger in these parts. It must be stressed that good weather is needed to fish many of the marks on this exposed coast.

Portscatho is invaded by holidaymakers in summer and all fishing should be confined to late evening and early morning. Bass, mackerel, garfish and mullet during summer and autumn, mostly on float tackle worked from the flanking rocky ground. Wrasse are about, but few reports of fish over 4 lb. Fine wrasse territory is, however, close at hand. To reach the water at **Zone Point** is a tramp down a cliff path and finally a climb over rocks to convenient ledges. Leger and float fishing with crab will take ballans up to 7 lb and these methods are also used for bass, but you need live prawn, sandeel or peeler crab as bait. Spinning with small artificial eels or metal blade lures which kick up vibration are good. Groundbait is an asset for bringing mullet in and there are plenty in this area. Bull huss to 13¾ lb were taken at night and more than a few good fish during daylight are on record. Leger a good helping of squid, cuttlefish or a cocktail laced with juicy worm.

St Mawes is an up-market, picturesque harbour-side village visited by summer yachtsmen, artists and writers. There is good mullet fishing, but finding a quiet spot can be difficult. Like all harbour mullet they are notoriously hard to catch. It is infuriating to have a fat 5-pounder ignore your float bait and then suck bread from a discarded sandwich. Mackerel flesh can prove a more attractive hook offering than bread, and maggot also does well.

Mylor Creek is also a good mullet area during the summer, but fishing is made difficult by the many sailing craft. Bass are occasionally caught before all the water-borne activity begins and in the peace of the late evening. Bull huss are prolific in the Falmouth area creeks after dark. **Trefusis Point** is approximately one mile of rocky shoreline spaced with sandy coves. The bottom and float fishing is excellent for wrasse, with fish up to 5 lb regularly showing. Spinning takes mackerel, pollack and a few bass mostly in the early morning. This is a good area for family picnics. In the autumn and winter ray and flounder are often about.

Falmouth has a pier and harbour walls at Custom House Quay, but both become extremely busy in the holiday season. It is essential to fish before the boat trippers are up and at the end of the day when the last mooring rope has been tied. It's mostly float fishing for mackerel, small pollack and garfish. Leger rigs occasionally take flatfish.

Pendennis Point is on the outer western flank of Falmouth harbour approaches. There's rock fishing for wrasse, but fish over 4 lb are rare. Reasonable bass are taken on live prawn float-fished at first light on the making tide. There is no shortage of mackerel and garfish on warm summer evenings. Large shoals of mackerel often pass the Point. The trick is to cast a spinning lure beyond the skittering fish and wind back fast through them. Float fishing can also be very productive.

Helford River, with its spread of picturesque creeks, offers everything for the mullet angler. Fish breaking the surface is often the only disturbance of the wooded inlets. Bass are active with the flooding tide, but most are little bigger than schoolies. There is good flounder fishing in the winter, but rarely does the Helford produce fish over 3 lb. Thornback enter the Helford complex in late spring and stay around until the autumn. Marks in the Porthallack and Toll Point areas are among the best. A ferry runs across to Helford Passage, dodging a few thousand sailing craft in summer. This 'was' smuggling country. Frenchman's Creek, made famous by novelist Daphne du Maurier, is one of many hiding between trees growing down to the water's edge.

The **Lizard Peninsula** marks the most southerly point of England. There are many fishing villages, including **Coverack**, which has an ideal harbour wall for sliding float fishing when the tide is well up. You can expect to catch mackerel, garfish and bass if you fish early or late. Mullet come into the area with the tide. The ground to the right is very rough and offers good wrasse during daylight and conger after dark. Sizeable whiting can be taken during winter nights. The churchyard at St Keverne, which is about a mile inland, reveals the great dangers of the Manacles Reef lying just offshore. About 500 souls who perished in various sea disasters lie buried here.

Porthoustock lies closest to the Manacles and fishing can be very good from the shore. All the usual species roam over the rocky ground. There are plenty of conger about after dark and big bass hunt among the rocks from half-tide up. Good spinning and float fishing for mackerel and garfish, particularly just after first light and in the hour before dark if there is plenty of water. Bull huss can also be expected to take a juicy bottom bait.

Cadgewith Cove is a rock fishing area mostly worked with the sliding float. Live prawn and marine worm are rated for summer fishing and fish strip does well late autumn. Pollack to 8 lb have been taken in this spot during the winter.

Lizard Point is very rocky with deep gullies and sandy patches often washed by heavy water. Wrasse are everywhere, but nothing like as numerous as they were due to netting for crab-pot bait, but a 5-pounder or two should show during a session to peeler crab bait. A good bass is a possibility on a leger bait placed on the sandy spots, with the best chance of a take being at the break of day. Conger and bull huss are active after dark and good ray are taken at times.

There are many good spots to fish between the Lizard and Porthleven. Well worth a mention are **Predannack Head**, **Poldu Cove** and the **Gunwailoe**, where a treasure ship sank in the 1600s. Valuable coins are occasionally found on the beaches. The cove marks the eastern end of **Loe Bar Beach**, where a gale-driven onshore surf is an awesome sight. Most of Loe Bar shelves steeply and is good for bass from spring to early winter. There is also reasonable fishing for ray, plaice, whiting, coalfish and pollack, depending on the time of year. Most of the larger small-eyed ray are taken at the eastern end, where the ground is less steep. Maintaining a bait correctly on the bottom in the violent water is difficult and it's usually anglers with the ability to cast beyond the main disturbance who score. So much ground is moved by the power of the sea that baits are deeply buried very quickly, hence the need to get outside the turmoil.

Porthleven is at the western end of the beach, where there is a long stone jetty for evening and early morning spinning and float fishing for mackerel, garfish and pollack. Legering could take a nice bass and some pretty big bull huss are about as well. Huge ground swells are a feature of the breakwater during stormy conditions and quite a few people have lost their lives to walls of water which arrive with great speed and strength. Vigilance is imperative.

Rinsey Head, **Cudden Point** and **Maen-Du-Point** are good wrasse and pollack fishing areas and many specimen fish are caught by local anglers. **Penzance Harbour** has several stone piers and harbour walls ideal for float fishing and spinning. Mackerel, pollack and garfish are the most likely species. The best sport for mullet is around Albert Pier, but you must have a drop net to get the fish from the water.

Newlyn Harbour houses the biggest commercial fishery and fish market in Cornwall and the water is well 'ground baited' by waste from the industry. Many species of fish are attracted by it and the most remarkable catch in British shore angling history was made here. The fish was a big-eyed tunny weighing 66 lb 12 oz hooked by Andrew Pascoe, a local angler, fishing from the

The region's tidal rivers hold specimen flatfish like this one

harbour wall. The battle between man and fish was long and hard and took place before an enthusiastic audience. Mullet are usually to be found in the harbour. Autumn is the time to think about double-figure pollack from marks between Newlyn and Land's End, which can only be reached with the aid of ropes which are permanently fastened to the steeper parts of the cliffs. This area is virtually a wall of rock stretching for miles and broken by small and picturesque coves, most of which are protected by a solid breakwater.

Mousehole old pier is a good mark from about half-tide up. Very rough ground covered by thick weed extends for some distance and sliding float tackle is the general method to catch pollack. Best fish on record weighed 12 lb, which is a fine fish. **Lamorna Cove** is surrounded by rocks covered by weed and there is a small stone breakwater. It's a fair area for mullet and there is reasonable bass fishing after dark and excellent sport with conger. The cove is privately owned and the rule of 'no rubbish − discarded line, etc' is rigorously enforced.

Penberth Cove has been used by fishermen for centuries. There is good float fishing from the steep rocks on both sides of the harbour for mullet, pollack and wrasse. Just a little way offshore local man Bill Chapple caught Britain's best boat hooked mackerel scaling 6 lb 2 oz.

Porthcurno beach, which is close to the famous open-air Minack Theatre, fishes well for bass during the two hours after first light on a flood tide, but a few specimens have been hooked at dead low water. Spinning and float fishing from the flanking rocks can also be good for bass, but the catch is more likely to be pollack, mackerel and garfish. Plaice and dabs are possible from spring onwards, but the best sport is in autumn and early winter. Whiting appear in late September and stay throughout the winter.

Pedn-mên-an-mere is much rated for bass between September and mid-November. Single-hook leger tackle baited with squid, cuttlefish, sandeel, peeler crab or a combination of cocktails can do well. Turbot to just over 4½ lb have been taken, mostly in the second half of the year.

Nanjizal is the last accessible beach on Cornwall's Channel coast. Small-eyed ray, some thornbacks, flatties, and wrasse are taken, and there's also the chance of a turbot. This small cove is flanked on both sides by rocky outcrops, which are used for casting on to sand. The configuration of the beach is constantly altering due to its exposed position. This is a dangerous coast and it would be foolish to try to reach many of the spots which could obviously provide great fishing.

CORNWALL'S BAIT BEDS

Ballast Pond Torpoint:	King ragworm, ragworm, lugworm, soft and peeler crab.
St John's Torpoint:	Ragworm.
Forder, nr Saltash:	King ragworm.
Whitsand beaches:	Sandeels.
Portwrinkle:	Lugworm, soft-back and peeler crab.
Looe River:	Ragworm.
Hannafor:	Mussel, limpets.
Fowey, Pont Pill, Golant:	Ragworm, crabs, sandeels; prawns in the harbour.
Crinnis beach, Carlyon Bay:	Sandeels
Mevagissey:	Prawns in the harbour.
Polridmouth Beach, nr Fowey:	Lugworm.
Caerhays, nr Porthluney Cover:	Raking for sandeels.
Penryn River:	Ragworm, peeler, soft-back crabs.
Helford River:	Lugworm, clams, razorfish (dig near the Ferry Boat Inn).
Eastern Green beach, Penzance:	Lugworm.
Larrigan beach, between Penzance and Newlyn:	Lugworm, ragworm.
Penzance harbour:	Ragworm, lugworm (stay well away from moorings).
Newlyn harbour:	Ragworm (local restrictions apply).
Porthcurno:	Scraping for sandeels at low tide.
Pedn-mên-an-mere:	Lugworm, sandeel, ragworm.
Sennen:	Lugworm, sandeel, ragworm.
Hayle:	Lugworm, sandeel, ragworm.

Guide to South Cornwall's bountiful boat marks

BOAT fishing along and off the coast of Cornwall is outstanding, particularly during summer and autumn. The much indented coastline, superb estuaries and long tidal rivers are complemented by many huge offshore reefs and a multitude of wrecks.

The warm waters of the Gulf Stream seep along the coast bringing warmth and an incredible array of species, including exotic tropicals. Believe it or not, fish like opah, sunfish, big-eyed tunny, trigger fish, and Spanish mackerel have been taken on rod and line from Cornish waters. Even swordfish and gigantic blue-fin tuna have been trapped in commercial nets. There are porbeagle shark cruising in Cornish waters and as summer draws near the thresher arrives and perhaps a chance of a mako, a close relative of the great white shark.

The blue shark is the backbone of Cornish big-game fishing. The season begins in early June and continues until the middle of October, by which time in an average season around 300 fish over the Shark Angling Club's 75 lb qualifying weight will have been caught and landed and rather more smaller ones released. A conservation 'put 'em back alive' programme has probably saved shark fishing in the area – so please ask your skipper to release your fish!

This guide starts in the tidal **River Tamar** to the east, where the small-boat angler has the opportunity to catch many species in the sheltered waters. Conger are available year round and only in periods of extreme cold is sport slack. There are many eels in the river and conger angler Roger Herity of Plymouth, who has taken many heavy fish, reluctantly cut away an immense eel estimated to weigh 125 lb that threatened to turn his 15-foot boat over!

The river is a standby boat venue and when the weather cuts up rough and charter boats can't get to sea skippers know that even in the river conger to 60 lb can be taken in daylight. After dark and during neap tides legered cuttlefish or squid bring even greater success. Of the many good marks, a deep depression in the seabed, just off the pontoon to the right of the **Torpoint Ferry Slipway**, is excellent. Another good area is adjacent to **Wilcove** and a lot of good eels are holed up near the centre pier of the **Tamar Bridge**.

The Tamar is also a useful thornback river. Ray begin to show in April and stay until late winter, but it is in the first two months that the best catches are made. The river record for the species stands at just over 18 lb. Legering at anchor off **Cremyl**, which lies at the entrance to the Tamar and close to Millbrook Creek, can be worthwhile. Peeler crab is the best bait. Tides run swift and it is essential to pick a slacker neap.

Penlee Point and **Draystone Buoy**, at the western entrance to Plymouth Sound, has a bottom of rocks covered by thick weed. This is a first-rate conger area and fish to 48½ lb have been taken in daylight. I once took a bag of 85 lb at the spot in bright sun and with no more than 30 feet of water under the keel of a small dinghy.

There is good pollack fishing in September and October during the back-tide period. The best technique is a sliding float rig baited with live sandeel, prawn or king ragworm allowed to drift away 100 yards or more and then retrieved slowly. Trolling over the rocky bottom between **Penlee** and **Rame Head** with a small artificial or live sandeel is good for bass and pollack, especially in autumn. A trace 15 feet long weighted with a Jardine lead should be worked well astern of the boat wash and engine noise. Large wrasse are available in the coves on both sides of the headland.

An artificial or live sandeel trolled in the early morning in the vicinity of the wreck buoy, which marks the resting place of the 7,000-ton Liberty ship *James Eagan Layne* in **Whitsand Bay**, will account for good bass. To maximise your effort watch for sea birds working over the surface. The bass could be underneath feeding on small fish.

Knight Errant is a big area of broken ground three-quarters of a mile north of the Bell buoy. It's a useful spot for conger in daylight. My log book records fish of 33 lb and 29½ lb on legered squid. Two miles out from Seaton Beach are the **Sherbeterry Rocks**, where bottom fishing over a neap tide takes wrasse and conger. Driftlining with worm or live eel is good in a fast tide, preferably up-channel, for pollack and bass. This mark is at its best in the autumn.

Inner Ranneys is where you can troll over the reef with an artificial or live eel for bass and pollack. Large mullet are about in summer but are difficult to catch. In autumn they will hit mackerel flake on float gear. A groundbait bag tied on the anchor rope is a big attraction. Bottom and float fishing close to **Looe Island**, not the northern flank, is good for a variety of species, including bass taken on live driftlined sandeel. Big mullet are always about in summer and autumn. A cloud of minced mackerel mixed with bread quickly brings many fish within float range.

Looe has lost something of its reputation as Cornwall's major sea angling port, which was built around shark angling. Today the charter fleet is much smaller, a direct result of inflation, and now there are relatively few who can afford to charter at today's rates.

Sharking is best when only three or four baits are out and this has led to many skippers giving up the game to concentrate on the more lucrative reef and wreck trips. For all this the port is still a major angling centre and a fair-sized fleet sails each day, weather permitting, from the East Looe Quay. All the major reefs within a 25-mile radius are visited and many good fish are taken, particularly by holiday anglers. Looe is not a long-range wreck fishing port and most hulks fished lie no more than 20 miles from port. The Shark Angling Club of Great Britain has premises on the East Quay and a very nice social club close by. Its walls carry a history of shark angling from the port and in Cornish waters.

Many species find their way into the pretty **Fowey harbour**, which holds deep water. Large bass are taken in the autumn, almost always on live sandeel during the flood tide. Grey mullet are very numerous throughout the summer in the harbour and far into the tidal river. The various creeks on the east flank are also visited by the species. A mile upstream, at **Bodinnick**, the narrow neck which divides the two sides is rated for conger at night. It is essential to fish a neap tide as the water motors through at a rate of knots — the slack-water periods make life a lot easier.

We now enter big flounder and good bass territory. **Old Sawmills Reach** is very productive during a making tide. A spoon baited with worm is much favoured locally and should be tried. Sport hits a peak in autumn and winter. Sandbars stretch across the Fowey in front of the railway sidings near Golant, where very big flounder are caught. The British record was set here many years ago with a fish of 5 lb 11½ oz and it is rumoured that even bigger flats have been found in nets. The Fowey is full of sandeels, a natural food fish, and I have had up to a dozen bass averaging 3½ lb on live sandeel during a single tide just off the village. All were taken driftlining from an anchored dinghy. The mouth, of the creeks fish well for flounder and school bass in autumn and winter.

Due south of Gribben Head is the **Cannis Rock**, which is marked by a buoy. It's long been a noted bass mark and live sandeel lightly driftlined scores during a flooding tide. First light has always been tops, but 7-pounders have been caught during bright afternoons. In the summer and autumn the Cannis is also

The highlight of a day's fishing. An 84 lb blue shark caught off the Cornish coast

good for big pollack. Best fishing is on a spring tide.

Mevagissey has long been associated with boat angling, and there are many excellent marks within a few miles of the harbour. The ground off **Chapel Point** is rough and covered by huge rafts of kelp weed, so float fishing, spinning or driftlining with a flooding tide is the method to take bass and pollack. There are fine wrasse in the area, but sadly commercial netting has taken its toll on them.

The Field is a group of rocks fished for pollack. The long, flowing trace takes fish to 12 lb, and occasionally bigger, in the autumn. Anchored fishing after dark brings conger and bull huss. Not far away is **The Bellows**, a reef that features a main peak rising to within 40 feet of the surface at low water. In keeping with other similar rough ground areas it is frequently visited by charter boats taking anglers on evening conger trips. Sizeable pollack may be expected between June and October. Not far out from the tiny fishing village of Gorran Haven is the **Gwineas Rock**, which stands steep out of deep water. It can be a dangerous place to fish when the wind is blowing from the south or west and great care is needed. Good for bass and pollack, fish during middle range and spring tides. Double-figure wrasse do come to the persistent angler.

Of the many wrecks lying off Mevagissey the *Silver Laurel* is just over an hour's steam from port. Fish it for conger, ling, pollack and coalfish, while cod can be found anywhere. At this hulk I once had four 50 lb plus conger in quick succession, and during another visit took three ling on a very heavy-duty paternoster tackle weighing over 100 lb. The rod with its cracked butt still stands in my tackle room! Whiting abound in the area during autumn and winter. Within a four-square-mile box there are at least another four wrecks.

Gull Rock is a noted mark for pollack, with bigger fish in autumn. Driftlining with sandeel or live prawn is a favourite technique, while the 'flying collar' rig also has a great deal going for it, particularly during the bigger tides. Conger, bull huss and, at times, ling can be expected.

The **Bizzies** are one of Cornwall's traditional rock fishing areas which hit form from June through to October. This is one of the few remaining areas where red bream can be reliably expected in the summer and with the onset of autumn the black variety are also a possibility.

The vast harbour at **Falmouth** offers plenty of species and sheltered fishing in rough weather. The population of conger is undoubtedly high, but fishing close to some of the commercial piers and jetties, under which the eels live, is restricted. The harbour is almost an inland sea bounded by high ground and virtually all the species common in Cornish waters visit it at one time or another. At the entrance is **Black Rock**, marked by a huge beacon, where conger, bull huss and bass are regularly hooked. The ground off **Pendennis Head** is rough and holds bass and pollack, particularly very early morning when a spring tide is flooding. Driftlining and slow trolling are the accepted methods.

Although very close to the shore, the **Manacles** is one of the most dangerous reefs in Cornish waters. Lying as it does, directly across the approach to Falmouth on its western flank many a vessel has come to grief on it. Jagged pinnacles of rock rise out of deep water, but a few dry out during low springs and it cannot be fished when the weather is anything but calm. On its outside edge lie several sizeable wrecks, where big pollack constantly feature, but there is also good sport with ling, conger, cod, turbot, plaice and bream to be had. Fish bass early morning with trolled artificial eel. Driftlining is a gentler way of fishing over the gullies and to my mind there is nothing quite like being in a small dinghy on a bright calm morning, while down below your live sandeel or prawn is doing the business.

The deeps of Falmouth Bay contain many wrecks, many going to the bottom during the last war. They all hold good fish and, in addition to the common species, there is a possibility of haddock, which do not feature to any extent elsewhere in Cornish waters.

Mounts Bay contains many good marks mostly fished by Penzance-based charter boats during the main summer months. Being so close to the open Atlantic and much influenced by the warming Gulf Stream, it attracts a large variety of species.

Carnbase lies close inshore off Penlee Quarry on the west flank of the Bay. It's fine conger ground at night and also offers sport with good pollack. It lies on the approach to Newlyn, a very busy port and the home of a considerable commercial fishing fleet. Just who **Tommy Kneebones** is remains a mystery, but the ledge or area of low pinnacles named after him lies about 250 yards south-west of Mousehole in line with Point Spaniard. It is a reasonable mark in autumn for pollack and there are good conger on the cards.

Runnelstone Reef is rated one of the best inshore marks in West Cornwall waters. It can only be fished when the weather is quiet and during spring tides it is difficult to hold bottom. The area is also subject to long swells. Target species include pollack, wrasse, conger, cod, bass and the possibility of bream.

There are six major offshore reefs in Cornish waters; the

Eddystone, which lies 14 miles from Plymouth and about the same from Looe, is the best known and much visited. Its popularity is fully justified because rough ground extends for several miles all around the lighthouse built on the highest rock, which becomes submerged during spring tides. The depth of water varies from a few feet to 25 fathoms, and it is all too easy to run on to a jagged edge of red gneiss, a particularly hard type of rock.

The reef is basically a maze of canyons, pinnacles, and tracks of open sand. 43 species of fish have been captured in the area, which has produced quite a few national and local records. Compared with years past, the bass fishing is relatively poor, but probably still better than can be experienced at many other respected marks around Britain. The fish begin to arrive during the spring tides of April and May and anglers plan to be over the reef as dawn breaks to get the finest fishing and most of the double-figure specimens. After collecting sufficient launce – a big variety of sandeel – a drift pattern is established along a deep channel a mile out from the light. Boats play 'follow my leader', moving with the tide while the eels work close to the bottom on long traces.

Light tackle is used and the trace, which must be at least 12 feet long, is carried down with ball weights behind the swivel. Barrel leads are not used as they easily twist and spoil the flowing action of the trace. The best type of rod for the game is a nine-foot uptider. Most bass attack the eel fiercely and hook themselves, although a swift strike ensures good hook penetration. Once full light is up the bass stop feeding and there is little activity again until early afternoon. This second period can be quite productive during the first two hours of a spring tide, after slack water. Last light is also a much rated time for Eddystone bass.

Big pollack roam the Eddystone and fish in the 20 lb class are regularly caught, although the average is nearer 5 lb. Autumn and winter fishing is superior. A pinnacle coming out of deep water on the south side of the reef is usually a hotspot for both pollack and bass during the flood tide. Conger provide many a thrilling encounter, even in daylight, but it is after dark that the big hauls are made. My best is 212 lb of eels, the best going 42 lb during a five-hour spell over a dead neap tide. Large cod, ling, bull huss and whiting are all taken in quantity at the appropriate time of the year on either leger or paternoster rigs. Red bream are a possibility from June and black bream show by late July. Most shark drifts begin about six miles south of the 'stone'.

A few miles away to the north-west lie the **Hands Deeps**,

The many reefs are home to pollack, like this 18-pounder

a massive reef with pinnacles rising in deep water to at least 60 feet beneath the surface at the bottom of a big spring tide. It is a year-round mark producing a wide variety of species, including many large specimens. In recent years rough ground has begun to rival wreck fishing and the Hands now rate one of the best areas in South-West waters.

Pollack of 25½ lb, coalfish to almost 30 lb and cod in the 42 lb class show the quality of fishing that can be expected. King ragworm is a great pollack bait in spring and summer, but in autumn and winter fish strip and artificial eels become killers. The reef is visited by anglers with their own craft, but the best results are usually from a charter boat with a skipper who knows the ground.

Phillips Rocks, to the west, is formed from three big pinnacles which hold pollack. The east side of the reef tends to be better for the larger specimens, while conger lurk in every nook and cranny. There's plenty of lesser species such as pouting, whiting and dogfish.

About eight miles south of Looe are the **Brentons**, a rocky spot with three large peaks named Dinsta, Little Browns and Little Ferney. There is a main ridge several hundred yards wide running north to south and this is where there's excellent pollack sport. Equally good for the species are the pinnacles to the north-east. Bottom fishing produces cod, ling and conger, and it's one of the better spots for red bream in summer and blacks during the autumn.

Hatt Rock is 10½ miles south of Polperro. It features two main peaks surrounded by rough ground spaced with sand. Live sandeel is a deadly offering for specimen pollack during late summer and autumn. There is general bottom fishing for most species and whiting always seem to be in residence.

Top reef mark off Cornwall could well be the **Wolf Rock**, marked by a granite lighthouse which is hit by terrible winter gales. It is only its exposed position, with nothing but the Atlantic Ocean beyond, which keeps it relatively safe from anglers. It can only be fished when the weather pattern is good, the sea calm and likely to remain so for at least 12 hours. Massive pollack, cod, conger, ling and coalfish have been taken here by the few anglers who have managed to fish it. Pollack half as big again as the national rod and line record have come from the 'rock' during winter. Cod in the 60 lb class have also been taken!

Index